BY ERIC ROBINS

AFR

IMAGES AN

A RIDGE PRESS BOOK | PRAEGER P

& BLAINE LITTELL

657432

RICA

REALITIES

LISHERS NEW YORK WASHINGTON

Editor-in-Chief: Jerry Mason
Editor: Adolph Suehsdorf
Art Director: Albert Squillace
Associate Editor: Moira Duggan
Associate Editor: Barbara Hoffbeck
Art Assistant: Mark Liebergall
Art Assistant: David Namias
Art Production: Doris Mullane
Picture Research: Judy Underhill

PHOTOGRAPHS BY

MARVIN E. NEWMAN

ELIOT ELISOFON

VICTOR ENGLEBERT

WENDY V. WATRISS

GIL ROSS

ALAN TERNES

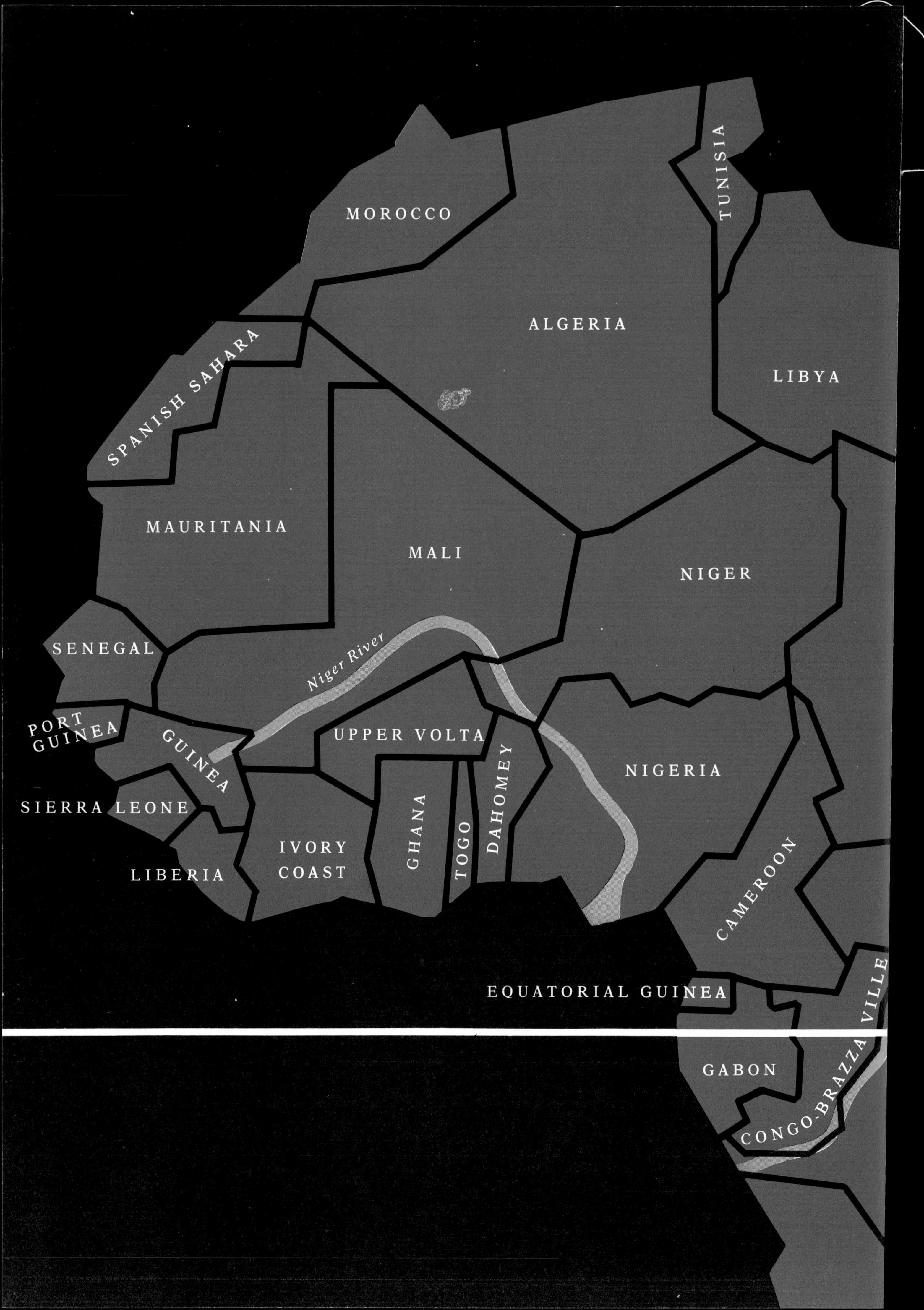
MOROCCO
TUNISIA
ALGERIA
LIBYA
SPANISH SAHARA
MAURITANIA
MALI
NIGER
SENEGAL
Niger River
PORT GUINEA
GUINEA
UPPER VOLTA
NIGERIA
SIERRA LEONE
DAHOMEY
GHANA
TOGO
IVORY COAST
LIBERIA
CAMEROON
EQUATORIAL GUINEA
GABON
CONGO-BRAZZAVILLE

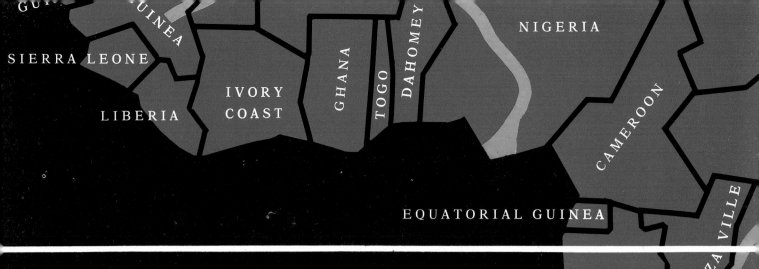

SIERRA LEONE
GUINEA
LIBERIA
IVORY COAST
GHANA
TOGO
DAHOMEY
NIGERIA
CAMEROON
EQUATORIAL GUINEA
GABON
CONGO-BRAZZAVILLE
ANGOLA
SOUTH-W
AFRIC

CONTENTS

CENTRAL AFRICAN REPUBLIC
ETHIOPIA
SOMALIA
CONGO-KINSHASA
UGANDA
KENYA
Congo River
RWANDA
BURUNDI
TANZANIA
MALAWI
ZAMBIA
MOZAMBIQUE
MALAGASY
RHODESIA
T
BOTSWANA
SOUTH AFRICA
SWAZILAND
LESOTHO

FOREWORD

The principal events which molded today's Africa took place between 1950 and 1970. Most importantly, these were the years which saw the white colonial powers deposed almost everywhere in Africa from the dominant positions they had occupied for a hundred years or more.

The governments and societies which have filled the vacuums created by the white withdrawal have responded variously to the problems and opportunities of their countries. Some have soared briefly on the rhetoric of fascinating leaders, then foundered on intransigent economic realities. Some have developed natural resources sufficiently to buy national stability. Some have established a political equilibrium. Some, out from under imperialist controls, have had the freedom to indulge in destructive tribal or religious civil war. Some, having ousted the colonialists, were unable to operate without them and have asked them back, risking loss of a measure of independence to acquire managerial talent, developmental credit, or support for a currency. Some have changed greatly, some not at all.

The authors of *Africa: Images and Realities* have sought to give a broad, legitimate description of these changes—or nonchanges—as they have affected this multiracial continent's varying regions, to provide a view of Africa that is general, yet pertinent and not too abstract. Their concern has been less for day-to-day events, which inevitably would outpace their text, than for pervasive traditions and trends, for fundamental characteristics, for underlying economic truths—all of which have determined Africa's past and will help to shape its future.

Not least of these influences are the incontrovertible facts of African geography. Few who have not lived long and traveled far in Africa can comprehend the vastness and grandeur of the continent, the fabulous wealth and incredible bleakness that have been lavished upon it. Across great stretches of terrain, the quickest route from one point to another is still by the slowest mode of transport—on foot, by tree-trunk canoe, on one of Africa's multitude of bicycles, astride a donkey, or atop a camel. Even a 600-mph jetliner takes the better part of a day to traverse the jewel-green, russet, sepia, and brown patterns of the land between the Indian Ocean and Sierra Leone. The color, texture, and physical quality of Africa are ably reflected in the book's many pictures—images and realities as relevant to an awareness of the continent as anything we say in the text.

For all its complexity, Africa has chosen its own route, and is embarking on its own journey into the future. It can no longer be described in terms of the self-serving policies of colonial overlords. As one of Africa's leaders has said "Our drum, and not the trumpets and bugles of others, shall be Africa's pacemaker." It is the authors' hope that this book will contribute to understanding of the images and realities that resound to the beat of Africa's drum.

Valuable assistance in the preparation of *Africa: Images and Realities* was given by Tom Little, an authority on Arab Africa; Marion Kaplan, a photojournalist who knows the continent intimately after a two-year trek through thirty-five of its countries, and Alan Rake, of London, who imparted his wide knowledge of French-speaking Africa. The works of Peter Webb, Africa bureau chief of *Newsweek*, John Hatch, and James Wilde of *TIME*, also are gratefully acknowledged.

1 REALITY BEHIND

THE MYTH

> **"Africa has, for generations now, been viewed through a web of myth so pervasive and so glib that understanding it becomes a twofold task: the task of clarifying the myth and the separate task of examining whatever reality has been hidden behind it."***

encompassed

by the waters of the Mediterranean Sea and the Atlantic and Indian Oceans, Africa—second largest continent on the globe—begins on the doorstep of Europe and ends five thousand miles later almost opposite Buenos Aires. The United States (which would merely form a broad belt across it), Western Europe, and India could be fitted into this geographical giant with room to spare. There are some fifty territories scattered over it. The differences from region to region, and even from country to country within the same area, are enormous.

One tiny sliver of a country, Gambia, smaller than Connecticut, bestrides the Gambia river for two hundred miles on its way through the sandy heart of Senegal. Another, the sepia Sudan, covers nearly a million square miles, which makes it nearly twice the size of Alaska, and Africa's largest nation. There is a vast area of desert in the north that once, ages ago, was green and fertile. South of this Saharan wilderness, half the continent is savannah, and between them, as well as in South and South-West Africa, is a semiarid transitional zone. There is, romantic legend to the contrary, no jungle. Jungle is an impenetrable tangle of undergrowth; what Africa contains, particularly in the Congos, Gabon, and several other regions of the west, is rain forest—a luxuriant growth of tall trees whose overarching branches form a canopy that excludes light and limits vegetation on the forest floor. Overall, the continent is poor in arable land, awesomely rich in existing and potential mineral resources, and spectacularly beautiful.

"She comes at you like an explosion," wrote Murrey Marder in the Washington *Post*, after accompanying the American secretary of state on a ten-nation tour of Africa in 1970. "Of colors. Of countries. Of customs. Of change. . . . No area of the world is more diversified or more in transition, with its mélange of feudal monarchies, revolutionary Arabic nations, supranationalistic one-party black states, 'people's democracy,' aspiringly 'humanistic' socialist societies and tribal federations with one foot in the twelfth century and another in the twentieth."

Climatically, Africa is subject to cruel extremes. It has life at its most fecund, and almost total sterility. Deadly droughts are followed by savage rainstorms which drown the land; some areas have less rainfall than Arizona, one is inundated with four hundred inches a year. A climber may freeze to death on Mount Kilimanjaro, the "roof of Africa," but at noon the moonscape rocks of the Sahara will sear a man's hand like a red-hot coal. The snows of the Mountains of the Moon in Uganda are within sight of the steaming "green hell" of the equatorial rain belt.

Africa is rich and threadbare poor. Ninety-eight percent of the earth's diamonds are mined in Africa and 55 percent of the world's gold. The principal mineral resources of the continent at present are in Morocco (phosphates, iron ore), Algeria (oil, phosphates), Tunisia (phosphates),

* *Africa and Africans,* by Paul Bohannan. American Museum of Natural History, Doubleday & Co., New York, 1964.

Libya (oil), United Arab Republic (oil, iron ore, phosphates), Mauritania (copper, iron ore), Senegal (phosphates), Upper Volta (manganese), Guinea (bauxite, diamonds, iron ore), Ghana (gold, manganese, diamonds), Nigeria (oil, tin), Cameroon (bauxite), Central African Republic (diamonds), Gabon (uranium, iron ore, manganese), Congo-Kinshasa (copper, tin, gold, diamonds, manganese, and half the world's supply of cobalt), Angola (oil, copper, diamonds, iron ore), Somali Republic (uranium), South-West Africa (diamonds), Republic of South Africa (gold, diamonds), Rhodesia (chrome, asbestos), Zambia (copper), Tanzania (diamonds), Ethiopia (potash). Oil seems to offer even greater promise, as new fields are tapped throughout the continent.

At the same time, Africa produces a mere 4 percent of the world's raw materials. Only some 10 percent of its 11.5 million square miles is currently arable. Eighty-five percent of its exports derive from less than one-twentieth of the land. The harsh earth, from which three out of four Africans make their living, is in many places tilled with plows whose design has not changed since Old Testament times.

The continent's present population of more than 350 million is made up of tribal and language groups speaking a Babel of some seven hundred tongues. There are some 60 million Moslems, most of them North African Arabs with closer ethnic ties to the Mideast than to black Africa. There are 40 million Bantus, a diverse ethnic group speaking several hundred languages and dialects, which inhabits most of the continent south of the Congo river. There is no average African. The skins of the continent's peoples range from white to ebony; in the center of Africa there are seven-foot-tall Watusis aboriginal pygmies, and tribesmen of Stone Age cultures who have not yet seen a wheel. By the end of the century, says Dr. Robert Gardiner of Ghana, the brilliant executive secretary of the United Nations Economic Commission for Africa, there will be upwards of 800 million Africans. "With roads and transport," he adds, "we are gradually making it possible for this physical market to emerge."

The emphasis of most African governments seeking to rise above a subsistence level is on development and cultivation of land, and on the improvement of transport and communications. Mighty dams have been constructed both for hydroelectric power and for irrigation: the Aswan in the United Arab Republic, the Volta in Ghana, the Kainji in Nigeria, and the four-hundred-foot Kariba wall joining Zambia and Rhodesia across the Zambezi. Yet, for many, water is so scarce as to be called "white gold," and children clear irrigation ditches with their bare hands to insure that none of it is wasted. The colonialists' dream of a Cape-to-Cairo highway has become a reality with the completion of a final stretch of tarred road linking Kenya and Ethiopia. But the 2,500-mile trans-African highway from Mombasa on the east to Lagos in the west is still in the planning stage in the seven countries it is ex-

pected to traverse.

Much of Africa has had less than a decade and a half of freedom from European overlords. Seventeen nations celebrated their first ten years of independence in 1970. Ghana, the first black colony to gain freedom, has been governing itself only since 1957. Some of the new nations, born in what is often described as "an explosion of sovereignty," have changed their names, preferring meaningful reminders of their African heritage to memories of their subservience. The former French Sudan is now Mali, after a glorious black kingdom of bygone days. Britain's Basutoland has become the Kingdom of Lesotho. Ghana, another great name in black history, has replaced Gold Coast. And French Somaliland is now the Territory of the Afars and Issas.

The footprints of the colonial explorers who trod yesteryear's "Dark Continent" —the last on earth to be investigated by Europeans— have grown faint in the African dust. Apart from the occasional weathered tablet or weed-skirted obelisk few memorials to their endeavors remain. The Catholic church tower in which Dr. David Livingstone's body rested in February, 1874, after his trans-African discoveries for the British, still stands at little Bagamoyo, Henry M. Stanley's starting point, on the coral coast of East Africa. The grave of John Cecil Rhodes, the empire builder, continues to be tended by a grizzled African headman in the windswept Matopos Hills, outside the Rhodesian city of Bulawayo. White-walled forts in the pattern of "Beau Geste," which have housed African slaves, German troops, or companies of French Foreign *Légionnaires* in their turn, stand crumbling in deserts and in the bush, and along the seaboards of mid-Africa. The green hills described by Ernest Hemingway, still majestic but somewhat less exotic, are on the main tourist route through northern Tanzania, which is traveled by thousands of American visitors every year.

"Darkest Africa" is hard to find these days. It exists only in remote corners of the continent, where old civilizations and cultures lie buried, where a native woman may still run screaming from a camera for fear that its evil eye will capture her soul, and where the only smog is a spiral of woodsmoke from a tribesman's fire. It is in the painted features of spirit-exorcising devil dancers deep in a West African forest, and in the solitude of a sandy cove on the Kenya shore where Sinbad the Sailor slept. It is in a fetid bell of branches and leaves where a bantam G'wi tribesman of Botswana prays to his hunter-god, the moon, for an exhausted gazelle to spear. It is in a Congo mangrove swamp where under a bruised sky the cry of a fish eagle pierces the humid silence. It is in the native songs and folklore which transcend the humiliations of colonial servitude and recall a rich past of noble kingdoms, wise rulers, and fearless fighting men. But Tarzan is nowhere to be seen.

What now plagues the continent's infant nations are the multiplex problems of survival in twentieth-century terms. Africa's leaders

—most of them earnest and able men—are retarded by the human deficiencies which also, unfortunately, are a part of Africa's heritage.

Poverty is one such "ogre," as African leaders call these problems. Personal poverty in terms of the world's goods is staggering for millions of Africans whose earnings are calculated in pennies a day. But there is as well the impoverishment visited upon the continent as a result of primitive habits and work techniques.

This is compounded by a lack of education. Lags in technical education are difficult to deal with until more progress is made in overcoming illiteracy. Statistically, about 40 percent of the world's adults are still illiterate. In Africa, where there is an unassuaged hunger for knowledge, the figure fluctuates between 80 and 85 percent. Although each year more children attend school in Africa, the population explosion probably will insure that the rate of illiteracy remains constant, and that universal primary education will stay beyond reach for many years.

Although the trend in education in free Africa has been away from the non-specific and clerical, and toward basic technical and manual training, there has been a temporary decline since independence in the general caliber of education. At the pre-college level there has been a drop simply because there are not enough qualified teachers for the bigger and often overcrowded classes; and there has been a decline in higher education because of the Africanization of universities and colleges —the too-rapid replacement, in several instances, of expatriate teachers with blacks who have not yet acquired appropriate academic credentials.

Learning by rote, the methodology of mediocrity introduced by the colonialists to insure moderate and "responsible" black Africans, is still retained in countries governed by whites. From time to time, Peace Corps teachers have tried to abolish it, yet resistance to innovation is immediate and comes, surprisingly, not so much from African teachers, as from the students themselves. They know that examinations and examiners exist solely to determine what the student has memorized. There are only two kinds of answers—correct and incorrect. For a student to think deeply is to waste the precious time he should be spending in memorizing the answers which will permit him to advance to the next grade, and eventually into one of the few advantageous jobs offered by the authorities. There is a terrible logic to all this which makes it difficult to envision the day when Africa will abandon it. Money and teachers, meanwhile, are too scarce and the competition for footholds on the educational—and every other—ladder too fierce to permit the luxury of experimentation and innovation.

Equally devitalizing are malnutrition and disease. The African worker operates at 50 to 65 percent efficiency, not because he is inherently lazy or untrained, but simply because he is not feeling well. He is almost certain to be suffering from at least one of half a dozen standard debilitat-

Three kinds of Africa: Ethiopia (opposite) is beautiful to gaze upon, materially well endowed. Mali thrives along nourishing route of Niger river (below), is sere and lifeless elsewhere. Tunisia (below right) has few physical assets, but flourishes through stability and progress.

ing diseases such as mosquito-carried malaria, dysentery, hepatitis, bilharzia (which is borne by tiny snails under the leaves of water-lilies), sleeping sickness (from the tsetse fly), or tuberculosis.

Unless he is fortunate, his ailments are aggravated by malnutrition, either because a better diet is not available or because he has not been taught, or refuses to learn, the basic elements of a balanced diet. He does not expect to live for many years beyond the age of fifty.

In Zambia alone, about four out every ten African children die before the age of five, mostly from malnutrition. Of those who reach school age, many walk five miles or more through the bush to their classes, sit through lessons, and plod back home in the afternoon without having had anything to eat. The vicious circle of malnutrition carries on into the adult life of the blacks everywhere in Africa. A poorly fed man has less working power, earns less money, and thus his children go hungry.

While tropical diseases still greatly affect the extent and pace of African economic development, they are being brought under control at a steady and satisfying rate. Important advances have been made in the field of health, most of them as a result of researches carried out by missionary doctors during the colonial period and later by teams of specialists from UN agencies. Smallpox, once Africa's most serious plague, has been wiped out in most areas. Means exist to attack and overcome widespread leprosy, malaria, tuberculosis, and bilharzia.

Less and less is Africa the graveyard it was for blacks and whites in the Victorian era.

Common to most African countries is the blight of tribalism. Although a dying force, it still is strong enough to pervert the struggle to build nations out of unstable territories. Tribal antipathies have flourished everywhere throughout history, but they were exacerbated in Africa by the arbitrary partitioning of the continent by the imperial powers. Boundaries were established regardless of the human upheavals they caused. Large tribes were slashed in half or, as in Nigeria, hostile tribes were thrown together. By such actions the seal of inevitability was set on the series of tragic and discordant conflicts which followed the eventual European withdrawal. Today different tribes and a host of cultures may have to be rallied around a single national symbol. The concept of a nation-state that embraces many factions, different ancestries, and several languages has to be constantly forced upon the masses, while a politician's visible tribal characteristics are keenly scrutinized by the voters.

African countries began independence with democratic western systems of multiple political parties grafted onto their constitutions, but tribalism has been the main factor in turning the majority of African countries into one-party states. Tribal and political infighting are reduced to a minimum, but unity is fostered at the risk of dictatorship. "Better that than civil war," say the supporters of the one-party system, which as a rule allows voters

a choice of several candidates from the same camp. Firm but fair, top-of-the-totem authority is traditionally accepted by Africans.

African intellectuals object to Africa being labeled "tribal" when every nation in the world has its group differences. Whatever the merits of such an argument, the terrible experience of Biafra may well have taught all of Africa an enduring lesson about the consequences of unrestrained tribalism in national affairs.

Some sociologists contend that the corruption which is to be found in varying degrees throughout black Africa—in one or two states it is almost a principal "industry," running down from the highest to the lowest levels of administration and commerce—springs from tribalism. They maintain that where lucrative business contracts with a nation-state to which he has minimal loyalty are concerned, a tribalist bureaucrat considers that his first duty in negotiating them relates to the financial advantage of himself and his family. He does not regard the regular acceptance of bribes as unpatriotic.

Population explosions, too, are of general concern. Whereas the world at large grows at an annual rate of 1.8 percent, Africa's people increase at a rate of 2.4 percent. At that rate her population by the year 2000 will be at least 768 million, as compared with 354 million for all North America.

The answer must lie in birth control. But effective family planning in Africa is a far distant goal. The infant mortality rate is still too high, the intrinsic social and monetary value of children still too great to permit vigorous or extensive birth-control programs.

It might be thought that in Africa, with its hordes of hungry and impoverished people, communism would be firmly established. It is not. The Russians and their rivals, the red Chinese, have edged into several countries through front and back doors, and remained at various levels of influence in the host territories. The Russians have been doing well in the Arab countries through supplying planes, armaments, missiles, and trained service personnel for the war against Israel, and they have established a presence in Nigeria as a result of the military aid they gave to help defeat Biafra. A revolutionary military regime in Somalia also has embraced them. The Chinese concentrate, with political profit, on helping the black peasants of Tanzania, Zambia, the Sudan, and the Congo-Brazzaville. Their biggest aid project is construction of the thousand-mile, $450 million railroad linking the Zambian copper belt with the big Tanzanian port of Dar-es-Salaam. In 1970 Peking also enhanced its prestige when it gained diplomatic recognition by Ethiopia.

Both Moscow and Peking have trained and equipped the African freedom fighters who make regular guerrilla raids on Rhodesia and the northern zones of South-West Africa, and fight in the anti-Portuguese liberation movements.

In Guinea, China and Russia fight a holding engagement—separately—

Africa's visage is infinitely varied. Below, from left: Samba tribesman of Dahomey, turbaned Berber of Morocco, a Congolese woman. Bottom: Masai woman of Kenya decked with beads. Tuareg nomad rests in tent in heat of desert day. Opposite: Carefully coifed, bold-featured Danakil.

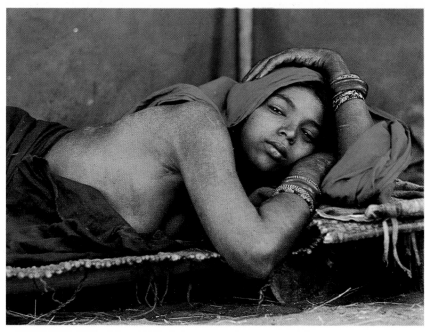

against western influence.

Russia has given university educations to thousands of Africans (as has the United States), whose kinsmen, incidentally, find both communism and capitalism alien to their established way of life.

It is the capitalists, however, who retain the initiative in most of sub-Saharan Africa, an international Tom Tiddler's ground where ideologies and creeds are constantly bent on consolidating footholds and eliminating competitors.

The nonwhite multitudes of Africa, of course, are bound closely in their hatred of the white men who control the republics of South Africa and Rhodesia, South-West Africa, and the Portuguese African territories. The blacks ask all major powers not to meddle in their domestic affairs. But they invite help in a unified fight against the "Pretoria-Salisbury-Lisbon axis" which, they say, could eventually inflame all Africa. There is constant racial tension where black Africa meets the explosive southern lobe of the continent. The Zambezi River forms the muddy boundary across which whites and black glower.

Conflicts between religion and color continue roughly just above or below the 13th Parallel, where blacks and Arabic peoples overlap. The Arabs, former slave-masters, are linked politically with black Africa in a facade of solidarity, but this is an alliance with little real meaning. In fact, the confrontation of Islam and black nationalism (which is laced with Christianity) may provide more fuel for future conflicts in Africa than tribalism. Cases in point are the large ex-French colony of Chad, where fierce bands of Moslem herdsmen have been trying to overthrow the black Africans, formerly their serfs, who are in power; the southern half of the Sudan, where for many years Khartoum government forces have battled black rebels; and Ethiopia's troubled Eritrea region, which Moslem guerrilla factions, backed by the Arabs and armed with communist weapons, claim as their own.

With the substitution of indigenous clergy and "African" church ceremonies for white missionaries and western ritual, Christianity is strengthening its bulwarks against Islam below the Sahara. At the same time, some four or five thousand breakaway sects with only tenuous connections with Christianity, are now evangelizing and increasing their numbers and influence on the same ground.

In the Ethiopian capital of Addis Ababa stands the headquarters of the Organization of African Unity, a tall, handsome brick-and-glass building. Africa Hall, as it has been named, is a symbol of an emerging continent which has brought its independent states together under one roof. Inside Africa Hall, near the huge, horseshoe-shaped conference chamber, there are large stained-glass windows which reflect an African artist's view of the continent's past, present, and future. On the left-hand window the days of slavery and colonialism are symbolized by a dragon and a black-winged skeleton. On the window to the right Africa's time of transition from colonial servitude to independence is represented by the slaying of the dragon. The center panel depicts a future of brotherhood, freedom, and progress.

The OAU was formed in Addis in May, 1963, and has established itself in a comparatively short time. It is pledged to nonalignment with power blocs, and to co-operation among members in the fields of education, economic development, communications, game conservation, health, sport, defense, and in bringing diplomatic, political, and military pressure on African countries still "captive" to the whites.

Like the United Nations (where it has an African Bureau), the OAU is sometimes the scene of heated disputes and walkouts by heads of state. It has been weak, and it has often had to labor to keep the seams of unity together. But, uniquely representing a conglomeration of peoples, languages, religions, traditions, customs, and political systems, it is slowly progressing and, like the UN, its members go on supporting it.

As an example from the top, tribalism is outlawed at the OAU and all discussions there are on a national plane. Several dangerous border disputes have been settled in Africa Hall.

With political freedom obtained, African leaders see the seventies as giving them the first real chance to attain economic independence. The emphasis is both on home development and a significant expansion of pan-African trade. In the next few years inter-African co-operation, with more and more economic groupings, will be the key to general success.

This fact is underscored by Tanzania's philosopher-president, Dr. Julius Nyerere, who has said: "We are all short of capital, and many of us are short also of the expertise which is just as vital to development. Each of our states needs to look outside for some capital investment. We try to lay down conditions so that it will not bankrupt us, but we also have to accept conditions. That is natural and inevitable. Sometimes they are conditions about the rates of interest, sometimes about marketing, sometimes about exclusive purchase from, or sale to, the 'donor' country; or sometimes they involve receiving goods which we can sell in order to raise development money. These are all conditions which we have to consider. We accept them or reject them according to their nature and our general circumstances. If we accept them, we do so knowing that we reduce our field of economic choice, our economic independence of action. That is the price we have agreed to pay. It is a deliberate and economic decision."

But then, he adds, Africa's republics have sometimes found that the aid, or the loan, or the personnel, was dependent on other factors they had not agreed to.

"We are told they will be taken away if we make a particular political decision which the donor does not like. Alternatively, it happens that when we are seeking support for economic projects we find ourselves being encouraged to act in

a certain manner because aid will be forthcoming if we do. At every point, in other words, we find our real freedom to make economic, social, and political choices is being jeopardized by our need for economic development.

"It is pointless to answer that we can refuse to sell our freedom in this manner. We all say that our nations and our policies are not for sale. And we do stand up against the most open and blatant attempts to intimidate us with economic weapons. But the fact is that every one of us agrees to little compromises here and there when we are conducting supposedly economic negotiations. We have no alternative. The world supply of disinterested altruists and unconditional aid is very small indeed. And however self-reliant we try to be in our economies and our development we are up against the fact that progress out of poverty has everywhere, throughout history, required some outside injection of capital or expertise.

"It becomes a question of how far we will go, and what kind of compromises we will make. We cannot refuse to make any. For our own people will refuse to accept poverty without hope of change. We must have economic development or we have no political stability; and without political stability we have no political independence either but become playthings of any other nation which desires to intervene in our affairs."

In a plea for more trade between Africa and other countries of the Third World, Nyerere declares: "Freedom and economic backwardness are incompatible in the modern world."

What then are the major tasks immediately ahead for Africa?

The expansion and modernization of agriculture, which represents in general 70 percent of the national revenue of African countries, is at the head of the list. An ungoverned expansion of industry would mean too many machines for too few trained black hands. And only agriculture can produce the savings necessary to underwrite that limited industrialization. This will produce those consumer goods which mean the employment of substantial labor forces, and for which both raw materials and markets exist locally.

Since the early days of independence, the prices that Africans pay for imported goods—some of them frivolous, but most of them essential items such as machinery, spare parts, tools, cloth, and so forth—have risen 10 to 15 percent, and in some cases more. At the same time some of the prices paid to the blacks for their raw materials and commodities have remained stationary or decreased.

In the postliberation black African states today there are too few indigenous intellectuals and specialists who can run things capably until a new generation appears. The rate of Africa's industrialization, therefore, will have to be geared largely to the numbers—and the pace of emergence— of young black African men and women (the latter

now winning their liberation from traditional servitude). Both are eager and able to play a part.

The seventies will, to a large extent, be a bootstrap decade for independent Africa, with each black government playing its part in bringing about economic growth. African exploitation of African natural resources has just begun with the basic business of processing raw materials, the embryonic stage of industrial development.

With more opportunistic white expatriates in most African nations than in the colonial days, Dr. Gardiner believes that "very little progress will be made until African countries can appraise their own problems and program and implement their own development projects. The biggest problem is the shortage of trained (African) manpower—not necessarily educated people, just people trained to do specific, useful jobs in commerce and

industry." (In early 1971 international representatives of 400 million Christians meeting in Addis Ababa decided that foreign interference was the most serious threat to the developing African nations.)

They will be needed, too, to provide new leaders in all spheres, and to build on the foundations that have been laid for educational advancement and improvement of living standards. They will be needed in the battle against malnutrition and poverty, and to foster the tourist trade, which often gives more employment and brings in more foreign currency than any other. They will be required to encourage millions of rural Africans to adopt new attitudes to labor. (In a number of countries the men sit by while the women do all the work in the fields and in the huts; in other places the men toil only in the mornings or afternoons.) Extolling production, cooperation, and marketing organization, Professor René Dumont, the French agronomist and author of *False Start in Africa*, states that "only the peasants can make the effort needed for underdeveloped countries to take off." The dedicated and ambitious young men will have to promote regional and subregional crops and, in the words of Dr. Gardiner, "make all boundaries cease to be barriers." They will have to be in the front ranks of what one observer has called the search for a society that should be both "modern" and "African."

Around the necks of the Africans as they struggle to achieve these things will be the millstones of aid which they have been unable, by force of circumstances, to throw off.

Africa is beset with formidable economic and social problems—not a few of them inherited from the colonialists—which represent a common challenge to its peoples.

"The mists of nationalist euphoria, the smoke screens of charismatic demogogy, the fogs of Cold War propaganda—all these have felt the useful blow and blast of many gales of argument and action," writes Basil Davidson, the British author and journalist who is an authority on African affairs. "The 1950's presided over the struggle for political emancipation. But the 1960's, whatever trials they have brought, have not been wasted. They have at any rate cleared the way for another and still greater struggle, a struggle for the fruits of political emancipation, for that new and unified society without which the peoples of Africa cannot even keep the freedom which they have, let alone enlarge it."*

The average African from Abidjan to Arusha has few material assets, and—as illustrated by a wrecking of industrialization in Ghana after independence—many inadequacies. Yet he has the will to work, at his own measured pace set by Africa's timelessness, for those projects that may bring a richer life to his people. He possesses a cheerful doggedness and a capacity for hardship and suffering which is free of any wish for revenge for the past. Such characteristics will be his chief assets as he reaches up to grasp the fruits of freedom in what may have been the original Garden of Eden.

* *Which Way Africa?* by Basil Davidson, Penguin African Library.

2 EAST AFRICA

A BLACK EDEN

on the edge

on the edge of the Serengeti Plain in northern Tanzania, in a desolate ravine baked by the sun and scarred by eroding rains, is one of the sites in eastern Africa where man may have been born. Known as Olduvai Gorge, it is at the site of what was once a small lake and is approached prosaically by car along a narrow dirt road, or by a light plane that lands on a tiny strip. The entrance to the gorge is marked by a straw-thatched hut. Altogether it is unimpressive, and one's initial reaction is likely to be keen disappointment. There is "nothing to see"—no massive, crumbling ruins; no giant, fossilized bones heaving themselves dramatically out of the earth. There is only a winding canyon cut through the earth's crust, its walls like layer cake. Some of the layers are red, some are gray, some brown, some blue. In the distant past all this was the shore of the lake, a lake which alternately rose and receded, each time adding another layer of silt and sand. Gradually, as hundreds of thousands of years passed, the deposits built up, augmented by ash and soil from the volcanoes nearby. The gorge itself is a comparatively recent occurrence —a geological bookmark.

A German butterfly collector by the name of Kattwinkel was the first to realize that there was more to Olduvai Gorge than met the eye. Wandering the site with pick and shovel, first in 1911, he unearthed fossilized remains of prehistoric animals. But it was Dr. Louis S. B. Leakey, the internationally known, Kenya-born anthropologist, who determined that Olduvai might, in fact, be the cradle of man. Certainly it is one of the world's great anthropological treasure houses, a natural time capsule literally bursting with ancient campsites and the stone tools and fragmented, fossilized remains of early man. It was in 1959 that Dr. Leakey found at Olduvai the first dramatic clue that humanity might have dawned there. He unearthed the skull of *Zinjanthropus boisei*, a 1,750,000-year-old apeman, a vegetable-eater who clung to life for a million years or so before nature decided he could not make the grade. Then Dr. Leakey found in Olduvai the bones of two individuals of the pygmy species *Homo habilis*, which lived alongside *Zinjanthropus*, but was more adept. Dr. Leakey nicknamed them the Child—born 1.8 million years ago and claimed by Leakey to be a direct ancestor of modern man—and Cinderella, aged only a million.

Earlier, Dr. Leakey had found in Kenya, near Lake Victoria, 20 million-year-old fossils belonging to an ancestral hominid which he dubbed *Kenyapithecus africanus*. Many scientists refused to accept Dr. Leakey's theory. They insisted that the remains were those of an ape. A common ancestor may go back 40 million years, and the point of departure for man and ape has still to be established beyond all doubt.

Olduvai Gorge—where the true father of *Homo sapiens* may still lie embedded below the present diggings—remains a Pandora's box for the scientific community as a whole. Dr. Leakey's finds at Olduvai and elsewhere tend to raise more questions than they answer, and Leakey's own hypotheses take commonsensible, if unexpected, turns —for instance, his explanation of the survival of early man in a hostile and predatory environment. From our current level of eminence we might like to think that our ancestors persisted through having greater intelligence than the beasts around them—by being able to fashion and use tools and weapons—or that perhaps they were simply endowed with a God-given supremacy over the other creatures of the earth. Leakey thinks otherwise: "It's been suggested that man, having come down from the trees, found himself in the world helpless and greatly in danger. I don't believe it. For one thing there's no evidence he came down from the trees at all. That's a myth from the textbooks. Man almost certainly comes from stock that never was in the trees. Being in the trees won't save you, anyway. Leopards take baboons out of the trees every night. Lions climb trees. Tigers climb trees. No, for me it's not that at all. I don't believe that early man ever suffered greatly from being the prey of carnivores."

Dr. Leakey has a way of talking about early man as if he were alive today, or talking about himself as if he were early man. "In my camp at Olduvai," he says, "I've had lions come and sniff at my head. I had a lion walk through the camp of two of my students, sniff at both of them, and walk out the other side."

Dr. Leakey wrinkles his nose, sniffs audibly, and adds: "Not food. You find there are man-eaters—lions, tigers, leopards—all through the books. And, of course, because they've eaten a man they're news. But they're rare: one in a hundred thousand. They're the psychopaths of the animal world. Either they're weak, or they're mad, or they've been wounded, or something has gone wrong and they take to human flesh."

A gleam comes into Dr. Leakey's eye. "So I believe," he says, "that the reason man survived in a very hostile world long before he could make real weapons and tools was simply that he doesn't taste nice, or smell nice—or both!"

Even today vestiges of ancient times still can be observed in East Africa. Among remote and primitive tribespeople antelopes still are speared with a sharp stake and the rock-rabbit (hyrax) brained with a stone.

Among the animals of the Serengeti, predation follows immemorial rituals. A downward spiral of sharp-eyed vultures, wide at the top and narrowing as it closes with the earth, points to the place where an animal has been killed. The kill has taken place in the early morning hours when there are few witnesses. The carcass is that of a wildebeest, a large, ungainly member of the antelope family, and the lions which have accomplished the kill—a male and two females—appear sated. They have entered their victim the easy way, through its soft underbelly, and now having eaten their fill, they seem bored.

Surrounding them like spectators at the scene of a traffic accident are the traditional scavengers—the vultures, marabou storks,

Sunrise at Olduvai Gorge, the anthropological wonderland in Tanzania, where excavations by Dr. Louis Leakey (opposite) have unearthed fossilized bones of several types of early man. Cruising, sharp-eyed vulture is link in immemorial food chain of animal multitudes of plains.

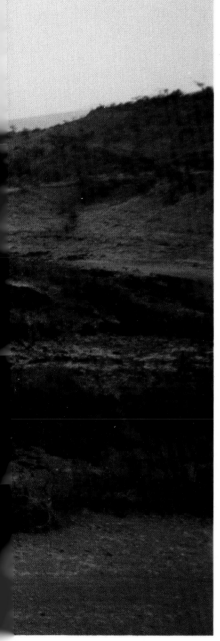

hyenas, and jackals. The jackals dart in and out, snatching at the wildebeest's entrails. A lioness swipes at them, but the motion is half-hearted, mechanical, as if the jackals were beneath contempt. The circle of bystanders edges closer, studying the lions. They seem to know that the lions are torn by indecision. Within them pride of possession wrestles with a deep need for sleep. At the same time the predators are growing thirsty. The scavengers are prepared to wait, knowing through instinct and observation that thirst will win in the end. When the three lions rise, stretch, and amble off to seek water and shelter from the midday sun, the scavengers move in.

At first there is bedlam and confusion—whirling feathers, snaps and snarls. Then order reasserts itself. Vultures whose beaks equip them for tearing flesh snatch their allotment, gorge, and then waddle away, too heavily loaded to fly. Meanwhile, the birds whose beaks are designed to break bones and scoop out marrow wait their turn. It is a macabre scene for the uninitiated. Yet a herd of wildebeest grazes placidly less than a stone's throw away. The fallen comrade arouses no sympathy. No memory of it remains, and by nightfall there will be nothing left of its cadaver but scattered bones, a skull, and some shreds of skin. In time the ants will take care of these.

Modern man is the intruder in these traditional and unchanged areas. But the pastoral Masai tribesman is very much at home. The Masai are Nilo-Hamitic, a term used to describe a complex of pastoral peoples including the Kipsigis (who today produce Olympic sprinters) and the stately Turkanas. The Nilo-Hamitics are one of Kenya's four main language groups, the others being Hamitic, Bantu—the largest section and made up of various tribes who practice agriculture—and Nilotic. The latter are of Somali origin and are to be found along the shores of Lake Victoria, stretching from the Uganda border well into Tanzania. Their origin can be traced by language and culture to the Sudan.

The period between the fourth and tenth centuries yields little documentary or archaeological evidence for tracing black evolution in East Africa. A ninth-century Chinese book describes the contrast between the wandering Somalis, who initiated the custom of drinking the blood and milk of cattle, and the "wild" coal-black natives of Mo Lin (now the Kenya coastal resort of Malindi). A tenth-century work places blacks as far north as the present border between Kenya and Somalia.

Between the twelfth and seventeenth centuries, famines, droughts, and wars caused mass movements of peoples throughout Africa. As did most of their neighboring tribes (there are fifty-seven main clans in Kenya alone), the Masai migrated to East Africa from the north, driving their cattle before them. Determined to enforce what they are certain is their God-given superiority over all other peoples, they kept a large standing army with which they elbowed others aside and seized great tracts of land. (Today Masai territory stretches across both sides of the Kenya-Tanzania border—15,000 square miles in Kenya and 25,000 square miles in northern Tanzania, with a total Masai population of around a quarter of a million.)

The Masai are cattle raisers with a strong, proprietary regard for their animals. They believe that when God divided heaven from earth he gave them their herds as a gift. From the cattle they extract meat (mostly on ceremonial occasions), milk, and blood, which they obtain by tapping an artery in the neck of a cow with a keen knife. The wound is afterwards sealed with a mixture of mud and manure. Blood caught in a gourd is mixed with milk to form a kind of yogurt. The Masai thrive on this singular diet. Medical men who have studied them say they are completely free of coronary disease, and they can run scores of miles without faltering.

In their deportment the Masai seek to emulate the courage of the lion. The custom is now banned by conservation-conscious governments, but witnesses who have seen young Masai *morani* (warriors)—smeared from head to foot in red ochre mud—on a lion hunt say there is no braver sight. Having tracked and eventually cornered a male lion, the Masai initiates encircle the animal. Then the bravest of the group rushes the snarling beast, brandishing his long-bladed spear. The lion charges and the young Masai attempts to impale it. (Retreat is out of the question.) Once his spear enters the lion, all are free to blood their own weapons. During this scene of violent combat, it is considered particularly sporting and courageous to grab the lion by the tail and hold on until it falls dead. On one occasion a *moran* whose right arm had been torn off by one swipe of a lion's paw earlier in the battle sat down and stoically watched his companions kill the beast.

The other tribes of East Africa learned to adjust to the Masai raiders and to each other. Thus when the Masai stripped the Giriama of their great herds of cattle, the Giriama—whose men now wear skirts—turned to farming on the steamy Kenya coast and became the traditional manufacturers of a deadly poison which other tribes bought and used on their spears and arrowheads. The Luo (the word means "swamp") came to Kenya from the maze-like *sudd* of the Upper Nile Valley and settled on the shores of Lake Victoria. They fought the other tribes in tight-knit phalanxes, their warriors protected by large shields and long spears, but they never learned to fight at night. Until recently they were subjected to periodic and bloody raids inflicted by their neighbors, the Kipsigis and the Nandi, who attacked them under cover of darkness. The forest-dwelling, honey-gathering Dorobo, who lived in Kenya long before the arrival of others, adapted to the newcomers and became spear- and shield-makers to the Masai, who were too proud to make their own.

More enervating than tribal conflict were the depredations of the Arab slavers. East Africa borders on the Indian Ocean, and the monsoons carried Arab merchants and adventurers from the Red Sea and the Persian Gulf to the African

Ungainly wildebeest, browsing elephant, bonecrushing hyena, striated zebra on go, maculate giraffe. Bottom: Pride rips off lions' share of Cape buffalo carcass. Hunters' leavings will feed complex society of scavengers. Nature maintains subtle balance of predators and prey.

coastline. They came in their dhows and built cities on the shores—Mombasa, Malindi, and Gedi in Kenya, and Bagamoyo in Tanzania. Their business was slaves and ivory, and in their relentless hunt for them they thrust deep into Africa's heart. The Masai held them off, but other tribes were made of lesser stuff.

In reluctant partnership with the Portuguese, who built Fort Jesus in Mombasa to protect their own un-Christian pursuits, the Arabs contributed to the balance of nature. With the slavers loose in East Africa, there was never any danger of a human population explosion. If the price in the markets of Muscat and Oman was right for eunuchs, the Arabs were prepared to kill fifty male Africans in an effort to produce a survivor. Hundreds of thousands of Africans were slaughtered because they were too old, too young, or too weak.

Obviously the slave trade, especially as practiced by the Arabs, could not go on forever. The English were among the first to help bring it to an end. And as they came, first as missionaries and explorers and finally as settlers, they upset forever the delicate balance between man, the land, and the animals that nature and the Arabs maintained over East Africa.

Long before their arrival, the coming of the white men was predicted to the Kikuyu people, Kenya's most numerous tribe. Also true to prediction, the strangers began in 1895 to lay tracks for their "iron snake"—a railroad from Mombasa westward to Lake Victoria. Although encouraged by a colonial under-secretary named Winston Churchill, progress was slow. Laborers brought from India by the British fell sick and died by the thousands.

The railroad's destination was Uganda, but a rude town was established in 1899 on either side of the tracks at the halfway point in the shadows of the knuckle-shaped Ngong foothills. The location—a mosquito-ridden swamp which the Masai called *nyarobe*, "the place of the water"—was less than ideal. Nonetheless, Nairobi became one of the pukka-sahib outposts of the empire, a bit of England in the wilderness, with polo matches, diplomatic receptions, garden parties, and point-to-point races, along with rigid social segregation. There was a section of town for the British officers, one for other ranks, a section for white civilians and their wives, and another for Indian laborers. Today Nairobi is one of the rapidly expanding cities of black Africa.

It did not escape the British settlers of Kenya that, in all of its 225,000 square miles, less than a quarter was arable, and of that only half was suitable for intensive cultivation. Most of that precious 13 percent of Kenya lay in the highlands that stretched north from Nairobi to the Uganda border. The whites swarmed toward this land. By tradition it was Kikuyu country. The British, ever sticklers for legality, did not seize it. They bought it from the Kikuyu survivors, who did not know they were deeding it to the strangers in perpetuity. Even if they had known, Kikuyu law forbade them to do so.

For the new settlers, the

Kenya highlands were everything their hearts desired. It was warm in the day, cool at night, and dew sprinkled the emerald grass with diamonds in the morning. It was high enough for pine trees, and the soil was rich enough for wheat, barley, corn, and milch cows. The English could ride to hounds here, and they did so just as they had at home, in "pink" coats, top hats, and with trained Africans for whippers-in. They were a colorful and headstrong lot, these white highlanders. The men were red-faced, good shots and hard drinkers. Their women were loud and bony. They prided themselves on being true pioneers, but the agronomists hired by the Kenyatta government after independence to study their methods were surprised to discover they had not been particularly good farmers. Their methods had been wasteful and often antiquated ("Don't tell me how to plant wheat. When I first came here there was nothing but Masai and thornbush!"). They did not have to be anything more than hardworking. Good land in the highlands was plentiful and labor cheap.

Those first fifty years rep-

resented a halcyon era for the semiaristocratic British trailblazers. A man shot the zebra and buffalo off his land to make room for the stock, and thought nothing —by Jove—of driving two hundred miles to Nairobi for a dance and then back again in time to greet the dawn and face another day's toil as overseer. Then, when planes started coming in, the thing to do was to fly down to Malindi for a weekend of big-game fishing and swimming, or over to clove-scented Zanzibar to haggle with the Arab shopkeepers for one of their brass-studded teakwood chests.

When they were not immersed in these activities, the white settlers were busy stopping game poaching and tribal warfare, starting schools for the *watoto* (African children), telling their mothers about the white man's medicine and modern clinics, and the grizzled, bowing grandfathers about democracy, money, and justice.

During that half-century, the population of East Africa soared. In Kenya alone it quadrupled, and there was a nagging land-hunger among Africans, especially the Kikuyu, and specifically for the rich highland fields which the whites had taken from them. This hunger erupted in the bloody Mau Mau rebellion in 1953, which became the rallying point for the movement which eventually swept Kenya to independence a decade later.

There were 7.5 million acres of fertile land in the old White Highlands. Simple justice, simple political common sense, dictated that an increasing proportion of this good earth be turned over to the indigenous population and, in the first few years after *uhuru* (independence), more than 2 million acres were bought from their former white owners and offered to land-starved black citizens. The process goes on, with the nagging—which no politician dare ignore—of a predominantly peasant African population of more than 11 million which is growing at the rate of 3 percent a year. The settlers' verdant farms continue to be chopped up—with varying degrees of economic success—into smallholder plots or larger co-operatives.

The demand remains insatiable, even with family planning and job sharing by two or three men. Appetites are whetted by the fact that just about half of the agricultural produce on which much of Kenya's economy rests—tea, coffee, dairy products, meat, and pyrethrum (dried chrysanthemums for insecticide)—comes from ranches, farms, and plantations that have remained in the hands of non-Africans, most of them white, who number one half of one percent of the population.

The pressure is great and it would be politically expedient to foreclose on the remaining white farmers. But, according to one of its own reports, wherever the Kenya government has done this it has cost the national economy "significant amounts of output, foreign exchange and personal income." The horns of the dilemma are sharp and, like it or not, the black Kenyan is obliged to admit that the white man—be he plantation owner, businessman, farmer, or tourist—continues to play a significant part in keeping the country's economic head, if not above water, at least close to the surface.

If there was anger among Africans over the continued white possession of so much land, there was fiery bitterness—with thousands coming vainly to the cities to look for work—regarding the ownership of just about everything else. For the commercial fabric of East Africa, from the ramshackle general stores in the bush to profitable secondary industries, did not belong to the Africans after *uhuru*. It was in the hands of East Africa's 400,000 Indians and Pakistanis, descendants of the coolies who built the "iron snake."

Almost everything about those Asians conspired to bring about drastic measures for curtailing their commercial power in East Africa. They had been told to integrate with the African population, and in Kenya to subscribe to Jomo Kenyatta's slogan of *harambee* (the cry of "Let's all pull together" which the crews of rope-operated river ferries address to their passengers). But religious scruples prevent an Asian from marrying outside his caste, much less marrying an African girl. They knew from long experience that their sons and nephews made cheaper and more efficient employees than Africans. And they continued to charge their black customers as much as the traffic would bear, and then sent their profits to banks in Delhi and London.

Tanzania first reacted to this situation in 1967. It forced out hundreds of non-citizen Asians, including Goans, and later nationalized scores of businesses, in the majority of which Asians had had a controlling or major interest. In Kenya, at the same time, President Kenyatta warned that, although those of any pigmentation who were "ready to join hands with Africans" were welcome to stay, non-Kenyans, however rich, who ridiculed the laws of the country, maintained "cat-and-mouse friendships," and insulted Africans, would be ordered to get out.

While mercifully not accompanied by the slaughter which marked the African overthrow of the ruling Arab minority and the erstwhile slave-owners on Zanzibar in 1964, the fatal blow fell swiftly on the Kenya Asians. Noncitizens—125,000 Asians had opted for British citizenship at the time of Kenya's independence—were told that their permits to stay and work in the country probably would not be renewed on expiration. Fearful of a flood of coffee-colored immigrants as a result of Kenyatta's edict, Britain decided that after early 1968 only 1,500 Asian household heads and their dependents would be admitted from East Africa each year. Clutching their newly-devalued British passports, 6,200 Asians from Kenya made it into Britain in a few panic-stricken, harrowing days before the exclusion took effect.

By early 1970, more than 25,000 Asians had taken part in the great exodus from Kenya to Britain, India, Canada, and to other parts of Africa. It is the intention of the Kenya government, faced with a jostling multitude of African unemployed, that in the end only its 60,000-odd fully quali-

Parliament building in modern Nairobi. Once a swamp in middle of railroad route from Mombasa to Lake Victoria, it became one of the pukka outposts of empire. Bottom: Hindu women of Kenya's dwindling Indian colony meet in temple. Opposite: Uganda's natural wonder—Murchison Falls.

fied Asian citizens will remain out of the original 185,000 brown population.

Kenya's example in squeezing out alien Asians was followed—but at a less vigorous pace—by her sister states of Zambia, the great butterfly-shaped land of copper mines and bushveld to the south, and Uganda to the west.

Reorganization and coordination remain the priorities of the hard-pressed political leaders of East Africa. However long and painful the process, the antipathetic tribes in each land must be welded into one nation with a single "paramount chief." In Uganda—a verdant patchwork of banana and sugar plantations, forests, and maize fields sandwiched between the Congo-Kinshasa and Kenya—officials are slowly creating a unified state after having stripped the country's four traditional tribal monarchs of their power. In Tanzania the government realized that limited aid from abroad would not provide the foundations on which to build a nation; its aim is to inculcate its 13 million people with a sense of common purpose in a socialist republic. Kenya is building luxury hotels and taking display advertisements in *The New York Times*, for in 1974 she hopes to be earning at least $110 million a year gross foreign exchange from jet tourists to East Africa's great natural zoos. Zambia's treasury is filled with copper riches, but both Uganda and Tanzania, endowed with scenic wonders, rely on the tourist trade to keep them buoyant and to assist the modernization of their basic agricultural economies. Given a continued lack of internal strife, the future of these countries, separately and collectively, seem well assured in twentieth-century development terms.

Outside East Africa's sun-drenched cities, ancient or modern, the problems are diminished. They take on a primordial quality in the bush, as if what is happening is somehow of less importance because it has all happened before. *Homo sapiens* (Caucasian or Kikuyu) looks at the "Red Indian" Masai and discovers that he is looking at him in much the way that *Homo habilis* might have eyed *Zinjanthropus*. Here, under this great expanse of sky, it is all so inevitable. Just as *Zinjanthropus* died out because his teeth did not permit him to switch to carrion when the droughts killed his roots and grasses, so those Masai who cling to a way of life that is no longer practical nor permissible will be eclipsed —noble savages out of step with time and deserted by the English who loved them for their classic beauty, their haughty intransigence and disdain for labor of any kind. But their fate is of concern to their governments. In both Kenya and Tanzania the Masai are successfully being encouraged to give up roaming and ruining the grasslands with their scrawny cattle. In ever-increasing numbers, they are leaping astride tractors, establishing wheat and dairy farms, running national parks and other wild-animal preserves, or joining local governments. Red ochre, wispy togas, looped ear-rings of multicolored beads, and matted pigtails have been banned to the Masai in Tanzania for several years. Instead, thousands of Masai men now swagger in the towns in creamy shirts, neatly pressed pants, leather shoes, and soft felt hats, indistinguishable to the foreign eye from other African inhabitants.

Yet it is the nature of East Africa to draw man to the past, to first principles, to the place where he may have been born. The answers are here, somewhere. As archaeologists prowl the Olduvai Gorge looking for fossilized clues to man's ancestry, other scientists have been searching for clues to behavior in the actions of animals of the forest and plain. Vast areas of Kenya, Tanzania, Uganda, and Zambia are assigned to game animals by the African governments, and each of the parks and reserves has something different to offer. Nairobi National Park is small (44 square miles), but its virtues are that it can be toured in a taxi after only a ten-minute drive from the city and that one will see most of the animals—elephant excepted—to be encountered on an extended tour of East Africa. In contrast, Kenya's Tsavo National Park is huge (8,034 square miles); but then so are its ubiquitous elephants, which paint themselves red with the park's dust and mud. Tanzania's Ngorongoro Crater, shaped like a huge, deep stadium, is spectacular, and so is Lake Manyara, where elephants can be spied through telescopes from the lip of the overhanging escarpment. The annual migration of great herds of zebra and wildebeest out of Serengeti National Park to new grazing grounds is almost Biblical in its splendor and as inexorable as the tide. Always there is more: the brutish buffalo staring out of the tall grass in Uganda's Queen Elizabeth National Park, and the sight of a stately Amboseli giraffe silhouetted against Africa's highest peak, Kilimanjaro (19,340 feet).

The scenery is overpoweringly spectacular. At night the stars seem closer to the ground, brighter and more glorious, than anywhere else on earth. The air is cool and clear, and the sounds—the shuddering roar of the lion and the staccato cough of the leopard—are electrifying. But these are only the backdrop, the incidental music. There is even more to East Africa, something indefinable, something awesome and hypnotic that tugs at the self-conscious like a half-remembered dream. Somewhere, perhaps beyond that patch of gnarled acacias, perhaps in the ghostly vapor that clings to a riverbed at sunrise, a deep and vital truth lies hidden.

"I had a farm in Africa, at the foot of the Ngong Hills," wrote Isak Dinesen in *Out of Africa*. "The geographical position and the height of the land combined to create a landscape that had not its like in the world. There was no fat on it and no luxuriance anywhere; it was Africa distilled up through 6,000 feet like the strong and refined essence of a continent. The sky was rarely more than blue or violet, with a profusion of mighty, weightless, ever-changing clouds towering up and sailing on it. Up in this high air you breathe easily, drawing in vital assurance and lightness of heart. In the highlands you woke up in the morning and thought: Here I am, where I ought to be."

3 WEST AFRICA: FROM

SLAVERY TO NATIONHOOD

the Gulf of Guinea carves a huge crescent out of central Africa. There are few natural harbors, and where the Atlantic is not dashed to pieces on rocky shores or bone-white beaches it loses itself, with ominous quiet, in the mangrove swamps. So, too, do the rivers. In other lands the rivers beckon man inland. In West Africa they barricade themselves behind savage rapids and then approach the sea with stealth, hiding their myriad branches in mazes of mangrove roots. Africa's third largest river, the Niger, meets the sea in this secretive manner. For years its true mouth remained hidden, while geographers debated whether it flowed east, west, south, or north under the Sahara desert and into the Mediterranean. Mungo Park, the Scottish doctor, found the true course of the Niger early in the nineteenth century by stalking it, hunter fashion, from behind (it flows slowly eastward before bending south to the Atlantic), but he lost his life in the rapids before reaching its mouth.

As a white man in West Africa, Mungo Park had the law of averages against him. Had he not died in the rapids, he probably would have been killed by warrior tribes, or else felled by disease, as were most of his companions. It was a practice of slave-trading ship captains to anchor offshore, or in the lagoons of the 14,000-square-mile Niger delta, to await the black middlemen who brought them their human cargoes. After sundown they kept their crews suffocating belowdecks, as protection against "noxious vapors." And during those nights and days of waiting, men died. It did not matter where they waited, whether in the Bight of Biafra, or on the other side of the delta in the Bight of Benin (home of classical bronze sculptures); every bay and inlet of the Guinea Coast exuded a deathly miasma.

Beware and take heed of the Bight of Benin
For few come out though many go in.

Forewarned but not forearmed by this doggerel of the times, the white invaders scouted the coast of West Africa in their sailing ships, staking their claims to the inhospitable coastline with forts of stone. The Portuguese came first, then the British and the French, the Swedes, the Dutch, the Danes, and the Brandenburgers. They built forts not so much to protect themselves against hostile natives (in most cases the natives were not particularly hostile) as to protect themselves against each other. But the forts, despite their thick stone walls and their batteries of iron-and-brass cannon facing out to sea, were no protection against disease. In the short space of fifty years the kingdom of Denmark contributed twenty-four governors to the old Gold Coast, twenty of whom died at their posts. Even after the introduction of quinine, even as diplomatic missions and consulates supplanted the crumbling forts, the mortality rate remained high, prompting the explorer Richard Burton to say of the recently opened British consulate in Lagos that it was "an iron coffin, containing a dead consul once a year."

Disease did not work singlehandedly against the white man. The heat oppressed him and drained him of his vigor. When the rains drove him indoors his clothing clung wetly to his body and the leather of his boots and the bindings of his few precious books turned green with mildew. They fell apart and so, in many cases, did he. Weak though he was through drink and fever, he was still man enough to want a woman. And on the West Coast the women were black. Each had her chief, and a father and uncles and brothers, with whom an arrangement would have to be made. If local protocol were spurned, there would be complications; it was easier to conform. Thus the white man fell into the rhythm of the life around him, with its slow but insistent and time-consuming demands on his thoughts and his energies. The cultural tie to Europe, already tautened by distance and the infrequency of mail and visitors from his country, rotted away with his shoes and books. Now, when those who spoke his language came by in their sailing ships, they found he was no longer one of them, but a man apart. Somehow he had become African and, thus, no longer useful—a figure to be pitied or scorned.

From Senegal south to Angola, Africa became known, for good reason, as the white man's grave. But if the West Coast was the Fever Coast, it was also the Grain Coast, the Coast of Elephant Tusks, the Gold Coast, and the Slave Coast. Most of all it was the Slave Coast. Slavery was a familiar condition in Africa. For centuries Arab caravans had crossed the Sahara with black-skinned slaves from the Sudan, and antagonistic black tribes often undertook to enslave their neighbors, although the conditions of their servitude were considerably less harsh than those of slaves in Europe or America.

The white man entered the business by making treaties with coastal chiefs. In return for muskets and gunpowder, glass beads, colored cloth, gin—whatever it was they wanted—the chiefs agreed to make war on neighboring tribes and turn their prisoners over to the European agents waiting for them in their coastal stations. The agents were known as "factors" and the establishments they occupied were called, in the euphemism of the day, "factories." From the *barracoons* of these factories or from the dungeons of the forts, the slaves (now branded and, in the case of the Portuguese, baptized) were herded into surf boats and swept by strong-shouldered African paddlers to the waiting slave ships. There were rumors that the white man was a cannibal, and many of the captives, fearing they would be eaten, hurled themselves into the sea and were drowned or devoured by sharks.

It was the vast sugar plantations and cotton fields of the New World, and their steady demand for cheap human labor, that brought the slave trade to its zenith. From the point of view of the white man and his material welfare, the slave trade was an unqualified success. Profit seduced morality, and morality in her shame remained silent. For Africa the slave trade, involving both Arabs and whites, was disaster. With tribe set against tribe, the centuries of slavery produced nothing but anarchy,

61

Aerial view of walled Nigerian village, near Kano, shows huts clustered on marginal soil such as that which supports most of Africa's peasants. Tragic tribalism of Nigeria pits Moslem Hausas, like tailor and turban-winding sultan's aide, against Yorubas (the drummer) and Ibos.

misery, and fear. The existing records are scanty, but it is estimated that as many as 15 million blacks were exported from Africa by slavers. This figure includes only those who survived. Perhaps as many as 30 or 40 million others were killed in the slaving raids, or died in the "factories" or in the holds of the slave ships. Half a cargo, three-quarters of a cargo, might perish and be thrown overboard during the run across the Atlantic—the slaver still showed a profit. There was that much money to be made.

The trade died hard. It was some years after it had been outlawed, first by the European powers and then by the United States, that it finally expired, in the second half of the nineteenth century.

The physical damage could be repaired and in time it was. Those vast areas of Africa which had been virtually depopulated by the slavers and their agents grew back again. Bellies were filled with manioc, the new tuberous root transplanted from South America; colonial authorities abolished tribal warfare, and medicine imported by white missionaries saved some of those who normally would have died. Tentatively at first and then by leaps and bounds, the population recovered and, at least numerically, became greater than ever.

Physically Africa recovered. But the mental, emotional, and psychological damage inflicted by the centuries of the slave trade were something else again. Those are wounds that have not healed. They are deep wounds and they are worn not by the African alone, but by his former captor as well. The blade of slavery, be it that of a Christian sword or a Moslem scimitar, cut both ways. For the white man it fostered a myth about the Negro which warps his thinking to the present day. Before the African slave trade came into its own, Europeans looked on Africans with a mixture of curiosity and awe. African potentates were received in European courts with pomp and ceremony. The conversion of an African prince to the True Faith assured a cardinal in Lisbon of an apostolic benediction from Rome. But the European slave trade changed all that. By definition, a master was the superior of his slave. Slaves, therefore, were inferior. Since the slaves being imported from Africa were black, syllogistic reasoning dictated that black men were inferior to white men and less than human. Being slaves, they had to be. Slavery ended, but the myth survives.

Certainly there were exceptions. There were and are white men who went deep into the bush, who learned the native languages and studied the ancient customs. But their findings were seldom passed on to those of their kind who made the big decisions. More typically, the white man who came to Africa as a slaver and then stayed on (suffering from postslavery guilt leavened by the suspicion that Africans must have been inferior if they allowed themselves to become enslaved in the first place) turned to the business of imposing his own way of life, his own system, on Africa; he had little time to spend on finding out what the Africans thought about it. In short, the white man came to Africa carrying his own yardstick—first to measure his own boundaries and then to measure the African himself. The results were of dubious value to the white man, and of no value whatsoever to the black.

The white colonialists were arrogant because they behaved not as guests eager to learn from their hosts but as conquerors and as exemplars of a civilization which would survive only if it remained uncontaminated by Africa. They wittingly practiced duplicity by bargaining land away from those who had no right to give it up, as they did from the Kikuyu "chiefs" in Kenya. They were cruel, as in the days when King Leopold of Belgium personally owned the Congo and the hands of Africans unwilling to work for him were chopped off. The Europeans were rapacious because their own chiefs in Europe were interested in immediate and not potential profits. Sadly enough, intolerance was the contribution of the missionaries. The Baptists were intolerant of the Methodists, the Methodists were intolerant of the Catholics, and all joined in an intolerance of the Africans' own ways of worship.

Few white men were guilty of all these vices, but most were guilty of some of them. Over the years Africans studied the pale skins for the secret of their success, and if they thought the intruders' behavior bizarre and unsettling, they seldom thought it evil. For them the traits displayed by the whites were simply expressions of power.

Yet black Africans have a far more complex and distinguished history than most whites have ever realized, and they are no strangers to power. In Ghana, a state controlled by a governmental structure existed as early as the fifth or sixth century A.D.—a period in which Europe was barely beginning to emerge from tribalism itself—and within another two centuries it became a kingdom of surpassing fame and authority which lasted for some five hundred years. The heart of ancient Ghana was located in the area between the Senegal and Niger rivers, in contemporary Mali and Mauritania, although its hegemony was extended over other black kingdoms to the south.

Ghana's eminence derived from its position astride some of the important trans-Saharan trade routes and from its exports—gold to Islamic North Africa and salt to the east and south. As early as 800 A.D. Ghana had an international reputation as "the land of gold," and the expenditures made by its nobility on lavish banquets for thousands of guests were famous when William of Normandy was embarking to conquer England. The early black empires of Africa—such as Ghana, and the Mali and Songhay kingdoms which followed it—appear to have been well organized. Although primitive in form, they had central administrations, a civil service, military enforcement of policy, and a system of taxation to support governmental operations. The accounts of travelers note with respect that peace and order were maintained over the full range of their territories.

The degradation endured

Lagos, Nigerian capital, is a turbulent mix of civilizations. It displays the technological advancements that contact with the West confers, and the rich, unquenchable cultural heritage of Africa. Right: Two kinds of water transport, both efficient. Below: A bazaar; tin shanties.

in the slave-raiding centuries, and subjugation by the rapacious imperial culture of nineteenth-century Europe, have served to dim Africans' awareness of their past achievements. Bereft of a heritage, they have been susceptible to a sense of inferiority, which many whites, believing it themselves, have been at pains to encourage.

Thus two civilizations—the white interloper persisting through economic domination, the black seeking to rediscover the past while finding a place in the twentieth century—confront each other in contemporary Africa. And where they meet, as in Ghana and Nigeria, neither sees the other whole. Today, Africa and Europe meet as if at a giant bazaar, bringing with them for purposes of sale, trade, and inspection their conceptions, preconceptions, and misconceptions, their attitudes, their hopes and dreams, their virtues and vices.

Mercurial Lagos is just such a bazaar. Lagos is the capital of Nigeria, Africa's most populous state. It is an international port, a center for trade and commerce. It has schools and hospitals, skyscrapers, traffic lights and traffic accidents—all the things that make a modern city.

Lagos spreads like an amoeba over the mangrove swamps. Her dwellings, unpainted, unlovely, and unplanned, push and jostle one another for a view of the street. Those too poor and weak to face the strong currents of the thoroughfares huddle behind their richer relatives in obsequious clusters, their rusting tin roofs joined together in common defense against the elements. Here in the backwaters, life is slower and quieter. The roar of traffic is shut out and the babble of voices becomes a murmur; shouts hurled into the air settle to the ground in phrases and then sentences. They are villages, these little enclaves, banded together protectively against the almost overwhelming world outside; villages with their old men presiding over the social order; villages with mothers pounding manioc in wooden bowls and elder children looking after the younger ones. They are islands of calm in a sea of chaos, the connecting link between old and new. The young clerk in white shirt and black tie, his hands stained with carbon paper and his sight blurred by endless columns of figures, comes home at night to these hamlets-within-a-city. And once again Africa reasserts itself. Because he is a wage earner, his money must go to support not only his wife—or his wives—and his children, but also all those with the faintest claim to kinship. The nephew of his wife's uncle, arriving in Lagos out of work and insufficiently educated to find any, can seek him out and demand his share of the pot. Earning more does not mean more for himself and his immediate family. It merely means more relatives and, if relatives are in short supply, replacements in the form of those who can lay claim to kinship by virtue of their connection with his family village, or even with his tribe. It is Africa's unwritten social-security system. It does distribute money, but it also saps ambition.

Lagos is not the nation's

soul, nor its heart nor its head. It is rather an appendage grafted onto the body of Nigeria to serve as a conduit for trade, a headquarters for the foreigner and for those Nigerians willing to meet him with the idea of doing business. "Most nations," says Wole Soyinka, Nigerian playwright, novelist, and poet, "hide their agonies and their crises, and try to protect their deepest values, in essence by wearing for the foreign intruder a clown's face; and for an international port especially, such a mask is inevitably a composite of the circus hats, the scars and other profanities of the nations who congregate in it. Lagos is the comedian's mask of Nigeria."

For Soyinka the "profanities" applied to the mask like coats of paint are imported. If not imported, they are cheap, homemade facsimiles of the foreign product, doubly profane because they degrade the makers. There is much that strikes Soyinka and the traditionalists as profane: the huge American cars wedged like ships in drydock in the narrow lanes of the city; air-conditioned skyscrapers; women's European-style wigs, and even the schools and hospitals which, all too often, seem to have been put there not to benefit Nigerians but to enrich the publishers of textbooks and the manufacturers of medical equipment.

And it takes "dash" to do business in Nigeria. Dash—a customary form of payoff—is the oil that lubricates the wheels of progress. As dash once passed from slaver to village chief, dash now goes to Nigerian civil servants and key clerks for permission to do business. It is dash that moves goods in and out of Nigeria. It is dash that heals the breaches in rules and regulations. Even if no law is broken, an infraction will be found unless dash is applied. ("Dash me, Mastah," says the smiling, uniformed policeman after he has given the motorist directions. And the motorist dashes, having been told that motor vehicle inspections are time-consuming affairs and that no car in Lagos can pass one without dash.)

Dash is standardized, and the knowledgeable know just who must be dashed and how much. Dash is fixed at between 10 and 15 percent of the value of the item involved, or the contract to be signed.

It took a partnership of black and white to create the venality that prevails in Lagos. But the partnership could never have flourished had not Nigeria been rich. What is more, there would never have been a Nigeria had not the British invented it.

In other parts of Africa, the European colonizers separated clans from their time-honored capitals and divided villages from their traditional grazing grounds. The once mighty Bakongo people were thus dismembered by the French, the Belgians, and the Portuguese, just as the Ewes found themselves split between Ghana and Togo. But in Nigeria the British did just the opposite, uniting under one flag a group of tribes that, by all rights, should have been kept apart.

Contrast between teeming town marketplace in Ghana and empty landscape of countryside is an extreme encountered everywhere in Africa. Panorama (below) is near Kumasi, center of Ashanti tribe whose rite of enstooling rulers survives in Ghana today.

As the British penetrated ever deeper into the interior of what is today Nigeria (always with an eye to the land and what grew on it and lay beneath it, rather than to the people who walked its surface), they discovered certain things: that it was huge (350,000 square miles, or roughly twice the size of France), that it was almost hopelessly far-flung and disparate, but that sense could be made of it if all were brought together. Cocoa could be grown in the west; peanuts, meat, and hides could be shipped down from the north. Oil bubbled on the surface in the east and was later exploited sufficiently to put Nigeria among the world's top ten oil producers. Separately the various regions would amount to little more than small-time states limping into the future on one-crop economies. Joined together, however, the regions took on an entirely different look. Unified, Nigeria became rich.

Although tribal differences were acute and the Moslem north was another world to the black lower half of the country, the British decided that the larger the pie, the bigger the slices. Representatives of fifteen major tribes and ethnic groups who journeyed to London before independence to argue in favor of the creation of separate states were brushed aside. Britain's pragmatism led in time to the bitterest of modern Africa's wars.

When independence came in 1960, the new Nigeria (which included the United Nations trust territory of Northern Cameroons) was presented by the British as Africa's wealthiest, most stable, most powerful, and most respected state.

Yet there were strong and ancient animosities among the nearly two hundred tribes of Nigeria which transcended reason, sanity, and the sanctity of an expanding gross national product. As independence dawned it was clear that the departing British also removed the Pax Britannica through which, by force of arms when necessary, these passions had been kept in check. In particular, there was no one to mediate among the powerful Hausa, Yoruba, and Ibo peoples. Hausas in the north, Yorubas in the west, and Ibos in the east—these are as different from one another as Greek from Roman or Arab from Israelite.

In the north, dry with the dust that sweeps in from the Sahara, live the Hausas. Together with the light-skinned Fulanis, they inhabit a world of the past, a world of emirs and palaces, of camel caravans and feats of horsemanship, of medieval pomp and splendor. They are Moslems, arrogant, pure, and insular, and when their thoughts turn outward they look instinctively across the Sahara to Morocco, Egypt, and the Sudan, rarely southward to Lagos. For them the marshes of the south serve as little more than breeding grounds for black "savages" whom the Hausas, in times not long past, either put to the sword or into chains.

In the warm and humid west live the Yorubas. Part Christian, part Moslem, part pagan, theirs was a land squeezed between the turbaned slave-raiders of the north and the fierce

kings of Dahomey to the west. To protect themselves against their traditional enemies they gathered in large towns and constructed intricate systems of commerce and culture. Complex and often devious, the Yorubas excelled in the shifty game of postindependence Nigerian politics. Lagos became their playing field, and they remain prominent in the corridors of power.

In the east, in the moist forests and bushlands north of the Niger river delta, live the Ibos. Fifty years ago they were one of Nigeria's most backward tribes. Hut dwellers, not town people, they practiced cannibalism and human sacrifice. But then came the Christian missionaries. The Ibos, abandoning their primitive ways without a backward glance, grasped eagerly at the new religion and with it the entire Protestant ethic of study, hard work, and thrift. Reactions to the Ibos are rarely neutral; to know them is to form strong opinions. To some they are frugal, loyal, industrious, and intelligent. For others they are clannish, shrewd, miserly, and pushy, easier to admire than to like.

The Ibos are a group-minded people. Through a process of group selection, young men are brought forward to be educated. The young men never forget their responsibility toward the families and the villages that educated them. Over the years, like ants building a bridge with their bodies so that some of their number can pass forward, the Ibos have pushed their favored sons into the great world beyond, to secure a foothold there and pave the way for more Ibos. They spread into the far corners of Nigeria, establishing themselves as mechanics, drivers, clerks, teachers, bank tellers, secretaries, factory foremen, and in all other positions that required education, industry, and skill. The western region absorbed the Ibos easily, and even in the north, in the days before independence, there was little resistance. The northerners, disdainful of practical education and the hours of drudgery required of a clerk-typist, were pleased to see the Ibos take these mundane jobs. But by mutual agreement there was little real contact between the two groups. The Hausas sequestered the Ibos in *sabongaris*, the "strangers' quarters" built outside the mud walls of their ancient and inward-looking cities. The Ibos accepted ghetto life without murmur. With the money they saved, they sent for their families and, often ruthlessly, squeezed alien tribesmen out of the jobs they held to make space for more Ibo relations. Theirs was a closed society and wherever they went they spent their money in Ibo shops, drank in Ibo bars, and banked their savings in Ibo banks.

It all worked while the British were around, but then the British withdrew. The Moslem northerners, lusting for power, took a census purporting to show that their population had grown from 17 million to just under 30 million in ten years—nearly half of Nigeria's total. Corruption, political graft, and rigged elections became prevalent in the largely northern federal government. The inevitable *coup d'état*, staged by the army, brought down the corrupt civilian government.

In a countercoup, the eastern general who headed the military regime was executed. As if on signal, the Hausas and Fulanis of the north broke into the strangers' quarters of their cities and massacred the Ibos whom they had so fervently despised and feared for so long. By the hundreds of thousands, these Ibos, knowing there was no safety for them anywhere else, fled back to their eastern homeland. In May, 1967, the bearded Ibo leader, General Chukwuemeka Odumegwu Ojukwu, then in his mid-thirties, announced that the oil-rich, 30,000-square-mile area which he named Biafra had broken away from the rest of Nigeria. The majority of African heads of state, fearful of tribal splinters within their own lands, roundly condemned him.

For the next thirty months the country was plunged into the bloodiest, most heartrending and savage civil war in black Africa's strife-torn history. It far surpassed the civil wars of the sixties in the former Belgian Congo, in the numbers of troops engaged, the devastating force of firepower, the pillaging and casualties among both troops and civilians. For every soldier killed in a Biafran forest, scores of men, women, and children—particularly young children—slowly starved and died under the tropical sun. When Ojukwu acknowledged defeat in January, 1970, the civilian death toll in Biafra was about 2 million and almost every horror known to human conflict had been repeated a thousandfold.

Since war's end the difficult tasks of reconstruction and reunification have been pursued in relative peace, with a relative lack of vengeance, with a relative degree of sanity. "To keep Nigeria one is a task that must be done," one government slogan proclaimed. By late 1970, Nigeria—under the leadership of the young and able General Yakubu Gowon—had launched a massive development plan for agriculture, industry, transport, and education. Aid and assistance from abroad, particularly from the United States, have helped to reinvigorate Nigeria, and a booming oil industry, in which government participation has been broadened, regularly contributes handsome revenues to the national treasury.

Yet bitterness and incompatibility remain to plague relations between Hausas and Ibos and other tribes still harboring ancient and traditional grievances, particularly in the so-called Eastern Region—Biafra—where 5 million non-Ibos resist and resent Ibo efforts to re-establish themselves. It will take more than slogans and more than money, but the hateful and fearsome differentiations of tribalism must be overcome before Nigeria will be whole again.

If anything marks the Ghanaians and sets them apart from most of their fellow Africans, it is their ebullience. Every African laughs freely, but the 9 million Ghanaians can laugh at themselves. And where the Nigerians' tribal heritage brought them sorrow and anguish, the Ghanaians made use of their past to rid

Mammy Wagons, Accra's colorful, pertly named jitneys, charge a modest fare. Patterned cottons woven in foreign mills (bottom) brighten West Africa, complete circle of trade for African raw materials. Apartment (opposite) is part of vigorous industrial growth at Tema, port of Accra.

themselves of an autocrat. The autocrat's name is Kwame Nkrumah, the most charismatic leader modern Africa has yet produced. Long after his downfall and exile, he remains part of Ghana. The threads of his personality weave in and out of the fabric of the country like the threads that are woven into the multi-colored *kente* cloth of Ashantiland. Some are dross, because he did much harm to Ghana, but some are gold because he also did much good.

He might still be in power today were it not for one fatal mistake. He conceived that his mission was to rally all of black Africa against the white man still ruling on her soil. In his determination to meet the enemy on his terms but on their battleground, in attempting to carry Ghana out of Africa, he grasped the trappings of chieftaincy without submitting to the customary restraints. Thus, he violated a sacred and ancient tradition. Almost anything else could have been forgiven—even his corruption on a massive scale—but in this scorning of tradition Nkrumah went too far.

In Ghana, the symbol of power is not a throne but a stool. It is seldom used for sitting, for this would imply that the chief was more powerful than his office and in Ghana it is the office—and its symbol, the stool—that is revered. The chief, after all, is merely human. In Ghana, chiefs seldom assume the stool through heredity. Instead, they are selected by the village elders, democratically, after much discussion and much consultation with the rest of the village. Only after a consensus has been reached is the new chief chosen and enstooled.

Ashanti custom includes all the dazzling ceremonial of a 300-year-old kingdom in the rich, cocoa-growing valleys of central Ghana. In 1970, the 2 million Ashantis anointed and enstooled a new king, or *Asantehene*, in the first such investiture in thirty-five years. In a secret room in the royal palace at the Ashanti capital of Kumasi, a fifty-one-year-old, British-educated attorney who had been Ghana's ambassador-designate to Rome, donned the gorgeous robes of the *Asantehene* and perched briefly —three times—on the tribe's solid gold stool. Later, wearing a cap and tunic of pounded gold tablets and held aloft on a litter by burly courtiers, the new *Asantehene* was enjoined by the throng not to act on his own initiative as a ruler. In chants and songs he was reminded that the stool was not a symbol of dictatorial power, but of the balance between the people and their chosen potentate.

Nkrumah did not heed time-honored warnings. He ignored them, breaking the commandments as lightly as he broke with his past. In Nkrumah's vision of the future the past was an encumbrance, so he rewrote it, distorted it, and came to believe his own distortion. He became as remote and isolated from his people as his white enemy had been. Having reached the decision that they had had enough, the Ghanaians destooled him.

On the day of his overthrow in February, 1966, Nkrumah was far away in China on a self-appointed peace mission designed to

halt the fighting in Vietnam. His people celebrated in Ghana's capital city, Accra, young men covering their faces with flour and talcum powder to signify victory and joy, while women took their brooms and symbolically swept the streets.

The echoes of that celebration continue to reverberate through the streets. Accra is a tonic of a city, an elixir for flagging spirits. It has its slums, its grinding poverty, and its open sewers. Yet it excites rather than depresses. The doors of Accra are always open to the visitor. In Ghana the visitor is a friend.

Too often in Africa when the stranger laughs it is supposed that he is laughing at Africans, derisively. In Ghana it is assumed that he is laughing with his hosts. The Ghanaians are not plagued, even momentarily, by the nagging suspicion that they are inferior, but neither do they insist that they are superior. They are a proud people but theirs is not a somber pride, and the line between dignity and pomposity is clearly drawn.

Their outgoing, friendly natures frustrated Nkrumah and his designs for their future. In an effort to galvanize the easygoing Ghanaians into action, he told them they must hate outsiders along properly racist lines. "Before the white man knew of 'civilization,'" declared the Accra-published *Evening News* of June 5, 1964, in a typical Nkrumah-inspired editorial, "we of the black race had already traversed the path. . . . Today we match with the whites in every achievement of human endeavour; indeed more often than not the black man trounces, pummels, defeats and absolutely confounds the white man and woman wherever the challenge is thrown, intellectually, physically or spiritually. . . . The black man is here. The twentieth century is the century of the black man."

The notion that they must despise the white man to inherit the twentieth century struck the average Ghanaian as absurd. The white man himself was too absurd to hate, and if he needed putting down it could be done in high style and without rancor. The white man was not put in Ghana to be despised, but to be played with much as otters will play with the stolid beaver. In Ghana the put-down of the white man is an art form.

Ask a Ghanaian to dinner and he may arrive a day late, smiling confidently. Or he will appear with seven of his friends. Or he will invite you for an evening of Highlife, the rhythmic, insistent national dances of Ghana. They look easy —a simple and repetitive shuffle in time to the music. But they involve using muscles and motions that the white novice does not possess. The effort brings sweat to his brow and freezes his happy smile.

Or the Ghanaian will take you to a "band concert" which is not what it seems to be, but is, instead, a rambling play with music performed in the open air by wandering minstrels. It is scheduled to start at 8 P.M., begins at 10, and does not end for five hours. The metal folding chairs become intolerably uncomfortable and the plot unfolds in

Twi, a local language, and thus is impossible to follow. The principal comedians, who play the parts of fools and knaves, smear their faces with white paint (the ultimate put-down). Afterwards the Ghanaian host is likely to take his exhausted companion to a nightclub for more Highlife.

Ebullience and the happy habit of laughter mired Nkrumah's dreams for Ghana almost from the moment he started dreaming them. His vision called for phalanxes of disciplined troops leading all Africa toward victory in a glorious triumph over the white oppressors.

He spent money with monumental recklessness. Prestige was the order of the day. Nkrumah built Black Star Square, a huge, asphalt-covered assembly ground dominated by a gigantic, vaulting arch of reinforced concrete containing a speaker's platform. Unfortunately, the platform was too high. The crowds could neither see nor hear the speaker. A second and more functional platform had to be constructed lower down.

For a conference of the Organization for African Unity in 1965, he caused to be constructed a multistory building containing sixty lavish (and bugged) suites, several conference chambers, and a dining hall equipped to feed 1,500 guests. Plumbers, carpenters, masons, and electricians, working in three shifts, toiled twenty-four hours a day, seven days a week, for ten months to complete "Job 600," as it was called, in time for the conference. The meeting lasted five days, was boycotted by many of the delegates, and accomplished nothing. The cost to Ghana was $20 million.

Compared with many of the African nations which did or did not send representatives to the Accra OAU meeting, Ghana is inherently rich. She is the world's chief exporter of cocoa and her subsurface wealth includes gold (which first brought her the name of the Gold Coast), industrial diamonds, manganese, and bauxite. But for Nkrumah, Ghana's prestige required industry and to this end he established forty-seven state-owned corporations. All but three lost money from the moment of their inception.

The steel mill erected at the new port of Tema was supposed to grow rich and strong on a diet of scrap metal, but there never was enough scrap to feed the machine properly. The cost of transporting an automobile wreck from Kumasi to the coast was prohibitive, and the mill was able to operate only a few months of the year. Similarly, a corned-beef factory at Bolgatanga fell prey to an entirely foreseeable and disastrous dearth of beef in the neighborhood, and the sugar refineries at Komenda and Asutsuare were built without provisions being made for sugar cane to process.

To carry the spirit and flag of Ghana to all corners of the world, Nkrumah sank vast amounts of money into the enterprise called Ghana Airways, and opened elaborate embassies in foreign countries. These were the public expenditures. More privately, he diverted funds to his Russian-trained security guard, to security walls around his residences, to bullet-proof Rolls-Royces—and with reason. After five assassination attempts, Nkrumah feared for his life.

Ghana began her career as an independent nation in March, 1957, with Kwame Nkrumah at the helm and $500 million in her coffers. Nine years later, when his army overthrew him in what became Africa's sixth *coup d'état* in a few months, Ghana was approximately $1 billion in debt.

Yet not even his bitterest enemies (and those of his opponents who languished in jail for the better part of his reign could certainly be called bitter) would say that Nkrumah was all bad. Much of the money he spent went to education. Although here again he spent too much and too quickly (there are too many expensive and elaborate schools and far too few qualified teachers to staff them), he did provide education for the many where previously it had existed only for the few. Nkrumah also provided hospitals, built roads, and lured and bludgeoned foreign capital (most of it American) into building for Ghana for Volta river project, which now provides power to manufacture aluminum and is to supply not only Ghana but vast areas of West Africa with hydroelectric power sufficient to their needs.

More important, Nkrumah —through personal magnetism, artful design, and sheer determination that it should come to pass— literally tore the heart out of tribalism in Ghana. In the six languages used by the announcers on Radio Ghana, Nkrumah taught Ghanaians how to think of themselves as one nation. His approach may have been roughshod. He broke the power of the chiefs and silenced those who opposed him, but it worked. Today most Ghanaians view themselves as a people, not a loose association of tribes, and in this respect they are ahead of most of their neighbors.

If there is still joy in Ghana over the destoolment of the tyrant, it is tinged with nostalgia. For Nkrumah, despite his many faults, was in his time the symbol of emergent Africa. There was no one quite like him. When he spoke, his was the voice of the black continent, and the white, brown, and yellow leaders of the world listened. Because he made himself important, the world powers beat a path to his door, bringing assistance and gifts, and urging him to become their friend.

"Poor, No Friend" reads the gilt script on the side of one of Accra's fleet of careering Mammy Wagons, jampacked with passengers who scorn a bus but are too poor to pay a cab fare. While accepting that neither the capitalist nor the communist world is ready to refinance Ghana along the profligate lines set by Kwame Nkrumah, the "Poor, No Friend" text does not signify self-pity. It is simply one of life's little jokes that the mirage of halcyon days faded with the eclipse of Nkrumah. And if the joke is a somewhat harsh one aimed at the Ghanaians, they know that the best thing for them to do is chuckle at it.

4 FRENCH-SPEAKING AFRICA

FREEDOM WITH STRINGS

by the end of the nineteenth century the partition of Africa was complete. The European powers had taken their seats around the conference table in the cold northern city of Berlin and had cynically divided Africa into spheres of influence.

France was given the largest area. Huge desert wastes from Algeria to Dahomey and from Senegal to Chad were soon to be colored purple on the map. In West Africa alone the French were to occupy some 1.5 million square miles, compared with the half million square miles which went to Britain. But British Africa was formed mainly from the coastal enclaves occupied by the early traders. It covered the rich, tropical lands, easily accessible from the sea, that had yielded gold, ivory, and slaves over the years. France was left with the pickings on the coast, unending miles of rough bush, and semidesert merging into the emptiness of the Sahara. In the colonial scramble for African land in the west of the continent, both France and Britain organized frontier delimitation teams to mark out the exact boundaries. Rivals by day, these European adventurers drove lines of wooden pegs into the arid savannah where Nigeria withers away into the Sahara. At night they invited one another to dinner, drank together and observed the formal graces, knowing full well that the other side would be up at dawn, possibly moving the demarcation pegs in an attempt to snatch another slice of African soil.

The Africans also had their say. Samory Touré, the warrior king of Guinea and grandfather of leftist President Sékou Touré of modern days, fought a long and tireless campaign from his strongholds in the Fouta Djallon mountains. In Dahomey, French progress was blocked by the local kings. But Conakry, Guinea's capital, fell in 1887.

In addition to the tropical enclaves, the French had claimed the desert and its fringes. This was where the Moslem Berbers from the north had been pushed out by the Bedouin invasions of the eleventh and twelfth centuries. They had crossed the Sahara and had mingled with the blacks, bringing with them their Islamic faith and their Arabized customs. The main French axis of penetration was from the coast eastward, through the "Sudan" south of the Sahara. This Arab word simply means "the country of the blacks." Far to the east was the Anglo-Egyptian Sudan; east of Senegal the French *Soudan* became the heart of French West Africa. The peoples there had mingled for centuries. They varied in color from black to almost white, and remained devoutly Islamic.

By the end of the century the French had hemmed the British into their coastal enclaves and the Germans into theirs (Togoland and Cameroon), and the artificial boundaries of West Africa had been set.

French West Africa then consisted of the *Soudan*, formed of part of today's Mali and Upper Volta, and also Mauritania, Senegal (the earliest French settlement), Niger, Guinea, the Ivory Coast, and Dahomey. The territories had been divided with scant regard for ethnic or tribal boundaries. Even today the Yoruba people are split between Dahomey and Nigeria, the Ewe people between Togo and Ghana, the Hausa between Niger and Nigeria, the Kru between the Ivory Coast and Liberia.

In Equatorial Africa, the explorers had opened up a great area of steaming rain forest where there had been little or no contact with the white man. Here a race had developed between the French explorer Count Savorgnan de Brazza, trying to gain the maximum amount of territory for the French, and Henry Morton Stanley, who had been commissioned to build an empire for King Leopold of the Belgians. Brazza acquired 500,000 square miles for France in two years. Stanley founded Leopoldville (now Kinshasa) in 1881. One year later Brazza proclaimed Brazzaville on the other side of the Congo river, to keep Stanley out of the French Congo. Stanley, in turn, promptly described Brazza's treaties with the native kings as "scraps of paper." But they determined the shape of French-speaking equatorial Africa as it has remained until today. This area covers four territories which in 1910 were grouped together as the Congo (Brazzaville), Oubangui-Shari (now the Central African Republic), Gabon, and Chad, in the north.

Once they had established their African jigsaw the colonial powers pursued basically similar policies. But the British and French systems soon diverged both in theory and in practice. The differences are expressions of the fundamentals of British and French character and culture.

A drive along the palm-fringed coast road from Nigeria to Ghana traverses the French-speaking states of Dahomey and Togo. More then ten years after independence, they still are pronouncedly French. The roads are crowded with Citroëns and Renaults; there are cafes advertising Dubonnet, and the African elite is stylishly dressed. The colonial menu, so uncompromisingly British in Nigeria, takes on a subtle French flavor. African couples in the average restaurant drink Chateauneuf-du-Pape or Vichy water with their meals. (Continuing imports of French wines and spirits add a serious burden to the balance of payments problems of the French-speaking African countries.)

The realities lie behind these outward manifestations. In theory the French system stemmed largely from the French Revolution, when edicts abolishing slavery declared that "all men, without distinction of color, domiciled in French colonies, are French citizens and enjoy all the rights assured by the constitution." The French wanted their Africans to become black Frenchmen. Those who made the grade—as *évolués*—presumably would be accepted on terms of full social equality. The British, with more racial arrogance, thought that Africans would not want, or be able, to become black Englishmen and that they should be left to work out their own culture. They slipped naturally into a system of indirect rule through the chiefs, while the French ruled through representatives responsible to

Sunbaked Mopti (opposite) lives beside Niger river in Mali, its narrow streets and blank-walled buildings appropriate to inward-looking Arabic temperament. Gao (bottom left), another river town, enjoys shade trees; nomads camped near Niger border (below) find shelter from sun in huts of woven mats. Bottom right: Mudwalled pen stores fodder for camels.

the central power.

French policy was to absorb Africans fully into the French culture. As early as 1848 some 12,000 Africans in Senegal became French citizens. Although they were mostly illiterate and non-Christians, they were entitled to send a representative to the French assembly in Paris. Nearly a century later, however, there were still only 78,000 French citizens in Senegal, and only 2,400 in all the remaining French West African territories.

The key to assimilation was education. French African schools struggled to preserve the same high standards as in France itself. Primary school education was given in French, and most French-speaking Africans today can remember being punished for speaking their vernacular language in the classroom. An Abidjan joke describes the African countries as "African-speaking France."

The French ideal was to teach not just a language as a medium of communication, but a whole system of intellectual and moral values expressed with clarity, elegance, and a certain formality. In theory, the African student in Senegal should be studying the same page of Caesar's Gallic wars at exactly the same time as a French student in the *lycée* in Bordeaux. The common culture was regarded as stronger than the divisions of race or color. As a result, the French managed to persuade the odd African to be proud of French culture. The British never seriously entertained a similar notion.

The French policy of total assimilation, for all that, affected only a minority. The vast majority was excluded from the rights and privileges extended to the *évolués*; for it the centralized French rule through the governors and their deputies was largely authoritarian and marked by forced labor and the suppression of individual rights.

And the French did not have a clear plan for the political evolution of the Africans. The rich French language has never had a word for self-government, and the idea of African independence was not even entertained by General de Gaulle at the conference of Free French held in Brazzaville, the wartime headquarters of French-speaking Africa, in 1944. The harsher forms of colonialism were later abolished and some reforms were made, but no fundamental changes were envisaged. Instead, at the end of the war, still more African leaders were invited to Paris. Among those who went was Felix Houphouët-Boigny of the Ivory Coast, later to become one of the most powerful and tenacious leaders of all French-speaking Africa. He had organized the Ivory Coast planters in the days when unions and political organizations were actively discouraged and frequently banned. In Paris he was joined by another outstanding African figure, Léopold Sédar Senghor of Senegal, a philosopher and poet as well as a politician. He had spent ten years as a teacher and government official in France, returning home to emerge as the most skillful political leader in his country.

Africans like Houphouët-

Sankoré mosque at Timbuktu has necessarily been restored, but looks as it did in 16th century, when city, now a dusty and forgotten outpost, was a jewel of black Mali kingdom—an abode of scholars and desert crossroads for camel caravans. Protruding timbers typify old structures.

Masked members of secret Dogon tribal society perform funeral dance. Unique, imaginative design of masks puts Dogons among Africa's finest artists. Below: Dogon village is set on Bandiagara escarpment of Mali. Block structures are houses, thatch-roof granaries are for millet.

Steel treads providing traction for wheels bogged down in sand are essential emergency equipment for vehicles that venture across drifting Sahara desert. These Arab traders pursue the heavily laden truck they have just managed to free from rut, somewhere in bleak wilderness.

Boigny and Senghor, who first sat in the assemblies in Paris in 1945-46, thought they would be rewarded for the part their people had played in fighting for *la patrie*. But the French deputies were still unprepared to make concessions to growing nationalism.

Back in West Africa, Houphouët-Boigny began the formation of the RDA, *Rassemblement Democratique Africain*, a party designed to represent the whole of French West and Equatorial Africa. At first the only objective was to secure equality for African representation within the French union (voting and representation were heavily weighted in favor of white France), but the party soon collided with the repressive colonial authorities. Meanwhile, in France, the African deputies worked closely with the French communists. The rising tide of black nationalism ran headlong into the intransigence of colonial policy.

The Ivory Coast was the scene of a series of strikes, boycotts and demonstrations which reached a climax in 1950, when thirteen people were killed and fifty wounded in a battle with the police. As the French stamped out political activity in the Ivory Coast, Houphouët-Boigny made a momentous decision. He broke with the communists and changed French-speaking Africa from a position of hopeless opposition to one of co-operation and pressure from within. From then on, he became a pillar of the French establishment, close to President de Gaulle and playing an important part at every stage of French African colonial evolution. In the late fifties came a major change in French policy. In 1956 Guy Mollet's Socialist government, with the help of Houphouët-Boigny, drafted the *loi cadre*, or outline law. This move was scarcely noticed in the Anglo-Saxon world. Yet in one bold stroke the center of power for African leaders was shifted from Paris to their own countries. It became clear that it was the end of French federal experiments in West and Equatorial Africa. Each local government began to concentrate on its own problems.

With Ghana's independence in 1957 and change sweeping British Africa, the French compromise was doomed. In 1958, President de Gaulle, reeling from the Algerian and Indo-Chinese disasters, embarked on a dramatic tour of Africa, accompanied by Houphouët-Boigny, one of his four senior ministers. He offered the twelve African territories in West and Equatorial Africa the simple choice of complete independence or autonomy in the French community with defense, foreign, and economic affairs to be decided jointly with France. In every state except one, General de Gaulle got a "Yes" vote by a massive majority for semiautonomy. The only "No" came from Guinea. Sékou Touré, the undoubted master of his own country, was twenty years younger than Houphouët-Boigny and had never become part of the Parisian political scene. His base was in his own country. A staunch federalist, he had long been a rival of the conservative Houphouët-Boigny. The antagonism between the two and Touré's doctrinaire Marxist stance made him reject de Gaulle. "Guinea prefers

poverty in freedom to riches in slavery," he told his enthusiastic followers. De Gaulle, in a huff, reacted by ordering a total French withdrawal from Guinea. The French-run civil and educational services packed up *en masse* after stripping their offices bare, even removing the typewriters and telephones.

Guinea, abandoned by Mother France, entered hopefully into a union with neighboring Ghana, then led by Kwame Nkrumah. But the fine-sounding idea was never to be realized. Only part of Ghana's promised $30 million loan to Guinea was ever paid. In the end it was Nkrumah who was to benefit the most. Several years later, in 1966, he was granted political refuge in Guinea, the country he had befriended in its hour of need. But autonomy within the French community was soon seen to be only a "rest house" on the road to full independence wanted by former French colonies.

By late 1959 Senegal and Soudan sought to come together and form an independent federation named Mali, after the ancient African empire. The French Assembly passed an historic and tactically sound constitutional amendment allowing continued membership in the French community after independence. Almost immediately the Ivory Coast and three of its neighbors asked for independence too, and one by one the remaining states in French West and Equatorial Africa followed. By 1960, today's French-speaking states had begun to take their final form. From then on, the federal links declined rapidly in importance. The big interterritorial

parties like the RDA shrank into their national frontiers. The experiment of a Senegal-Mali Federation collapsed within three months; the Ghana-Guinea union came to nothing. It was the hour of unbridled nationalism. Each country in French-speaking black Africa was to go its own way, becoming increasingly parochial in its outlook. And these new states were reborn within boundaries that had scarcely altered since the colonial grab for Africa. The only real changes were that the British West Cameroon voted to join its larger French neighbor, and British Togoland chose union with Ghana.

Currently the only unions to work are those based on necessity (as when the landlocked states of Upper Volta and Niger need some accommodation with the peoples of the coast), or on self-interest (as in the case of the Central African Customs and Economics Union formed by Congo-Brazzaville, the Central African Republic, Gabon, and Cameroon). It is only now, after more than a decade of painful experiment, that real progress is being made with economic unions.

Ironically, it was the old colonial power which held French-speaking Africa together in the early years of independence. The young African governments, determined to preserve stability and standards at all costs, needed more rather than fewer French administrators in the first few years, especially as the few educated and sophisticated Africans available went into politics. A Senegalese journalist who went to Nigeria for the first time at the end of the Biafran war in 1970, years after his own country's independence, came away with one vivid impression. It was not of the hosts of starving Biafran babies he had seen, but, as he said, of "those Nigerians really running their own country." He added: "There were no colonialists standing at their elbows, or even lurking in the shadows!" His contrast was with much of French-speaking Africa, still highly dependent on large numbers of French officials and pressured by Paris on important issues. French educational establishments today take about four thousand African students a year, and other institutes and businesses a further three thousand trainees.

The French have also played a prominent role in forming the African national armies, selling arms, incidentally, to both black- and white-ruled countries in Africa. These national forces were once part of the French colonial army. However, after independence each state had to build its own army, which it did with French personnel in a web of interlocking defense accords signed in 1960-61. There are some highly mobile French parachute and other regiments that can be moved back into Africa at the whisper of trouble. Reluctant though African leaders are to allow the French powers of military intervention, they are all too aware that their personal safety might depend on French protection in an attempted *coup*.

At least three former French African states—Guinea, Mali, and most recently Congo-Brazzaville—have tried to jettison French influence and to follow socialist-oriented policies of their own. It is not difficult to engender the right political atmosphere. Within a short period any party youth movement can make its mark, especially in the towns. Press, radio, and other means of mass communication are state-controlled and can be devoted to the ideological revolution. Trade unions and the ruling party itself reinforce the chosen trend. Yet each new government arising from a *coup* and seeking to go it alone is faced inescapably with the same economic and political realities as its predecessor. Despite a militant stance, each becomes afraid to push the French too far or run the risk of losing French aid. There is a show of revolution, and fiery proclamations, but the French ties remain, though they weaken with every passing year.

French influence on African economies has been of considerable importance. Political freedom has exposed the inability of most former French dependencies either to support themselves economically and financially or to operate themselves administratively. Since the outline and structure of each country had served only an aggressive imperial design, there was little on which to base solid growth. Arbitrary boundaries had created countries without the balanced resources on which development depends, and disharmony had been engendered among disparate peoples thus lumped together. As a result, most French-speaking African countries have been heavily dependent on French budget subvention, massive financial and technical aid pro-

Though shallow and diminishing, Lake Chad is vital to waterless regions of Cameroon, Chad, and Nigeria which encircle it. Its shores (below) are fertile, it can be fished by bamboo canoe. Beyond is desolation. Opposite: Woman and two daughters live in Borkou desert of northern Chad.

grams, and purchases of basic cash crops, like cocoa, peanuts, and coffee, at subsidized prices above world market levels. French monetary control in the franc zone is almost total. All foreign exchange earned by African countries is kept in the *Banque de Paris* in France. In exchange, the African franc, still called the CFA (*Colonies Françaises d'Afrique*) franc, is wholly convertible into French currency. Countries like Guinea and Mali, which tried to run their own currencies (with international and communist support) eventually gave up the unequal struggle and begged France for readmission to "the money club."

The franc zone is not just a question of monetary collaboration; it is a complete system of economic and financial assistance. It allows the free transfer of French capital in and out of Africa. It has greatly assisted the vast French investment in the Ivory Coast, Gabon, and to a lesser extent in Cameroon, Congo-Brazzaville, and Senegal. While the central banks in English-speaking African countries have a few white technical advisers, the regional banks in French-speaking West and Equatorial Africa have French government representatives making up between a third and a half of the members of their boards. When Britain devalued in late 1967, most of the English-speaking African states were organized on a sufficiently independent basis to follow their own destinies and ignore the British lead. But when France decided to devalue in 1958, and again in 1969, there was no prior consultation with the African members of the franc zone, who com-

plained bitterly at having their monetary policies entirely dependent on the exigencies of France's internal needs. When these African countries have wanted to devalue their own grossly overvalued currencies, they have been unable to do so. No country within the franc zone has changed its exchange rate since independence without acting in conjunction with France.

The franc system, of course, affords considerable protection to French investors and also provides a means of keeping "foreigners" out of the French African market. Newcomers to commercial Africa since the war, like the U.S., Italy, and Japan, have made much more progress in the traditionally free-trading British areas than in French-speaking Africa. Even France's Common Market partners, who have been called upon to shoulder a good proportion of French aid to the African continent, complain about the difficulties of extending their African trade. But for African countries it is the sheer volume of French aid that provides the strongest tie to France. Take, for example, the case of Senegal, the most economically advanced and the most promising French-speaking state at the time of independence. In the last decade, though making good progress in industrialization, it has been unable to grow enough foodstuffs to keep down its import bills. It is estimated that out of every three dollars of revenue from exports, two dollars are immediately used to pay for food imports. And this in a world where the value of manufactures is rising in proportion to the value of tropical agricultural products which provide

Racing dugouts on White Volta river pass modern building in Abidjan, Upper Volta capital. Nigerian money changer located at Cameroon border counts his wares. Street vendor in Dahomey (opposite) awaits customers for stock of foreign package goods and local fruits and vegetables.

Dahomey: Lake Dwellers live in bamboo stilt houses at Ganvie, fish the shallow, freshwater lagoons for food, and trade surplus. Long a tourist attraction, Lake Dwellers are threatened by salt-water contamination caused by new harbor jetties at nearby Cotonou, the commercial capital.

the bulk of the revenues of most African countries.

The Senegalese government spent 35 billion CFA francs in 1964-65 and 47 percent of this was required to pay the salaries of its civil servants. The Plan and Finances Commission pointed out that the country was spending twice as much on salaries as on operating and maintenance costs. In the Ivory Coast 15,000 civil servants, less than one half of one percent of the total population, have been getting 58 percent of the total budget. These abnormally high standards of living, compared with mass poverty, are features of other parts of black Africa, too, but in the French-speaking countries disproportionately high military costs must also be added. Imports of wines, spirits, and private cars are double the amounts spent on fertilizers, agricultural equipment, tractors, machinery, and tools.

Despite these economic excesses, the Ivory Coast has made spectacular economic progress, growing at a rate of 8 percent a year throughout the 1960's. This is partially the result of a flourishing production of virtually every cash and food crop known to Africa, particularly cocoa and a coffee well-suited for instant mixes, and partially from foreign investment—mostly French—in French-run processing and assembly plants.

Gabon is the other economic bright spot among former French territories. About the size of Colorado, but with less than half a million people, Gabon earns handsome profits from its agricultural products and the valuable hardwoods of its dense forests. Now it stands to benefit from proved and as yet unexploited reserves of oil, iron ore, and manganese which may make it one of the rich small nations of the world.

Gabon is also one of the areas of Africa that approximates the notions of people who have never been there. It sits on the equator, three-quarters covered by lush, luxuriant forest, the rest by grassland where herds of elephant browse.

The neighboring countries of Cameroon, Central African Republic, and Congo-Brazzaville are similarly endowed with rain forest and savannah, as are the Ivory Coast and Guinea, farther along on the western bulge of the continent. These countries have in varying degrees the usual mix of economic factors: crops raised by primitive subsistence farmers; the possibility of great wealth in subsurface minerals; trade imbalances serious enough to shake the foundations of government, and natural disadvantages—poor roads, unnavigable rivers, remoteness from a seaport—that require foreign money and technology to overcome.

Cameroon, named by the Portuguese after its exemplary shrimp (camaroes) and subsequently run by the Germans (Kamerun) and the British, as well as the French (Cameroun) is better off than most. It has the crops, the undeveloped mineral (bauxite), has direct access to the sea, and is blessed with a developmental plan generally agreed to be first-rate.

Plans for the CAR also are

well established, but will not soon bear fruit. This landlocked home of eighty ethnic groups suffers from all the traditional lacks of education, technical skill, transportation, and adequate government revenues.

The Congo-Brazzaville has been hospitable to the Chinese communists, although the French continue to operate most of its industry. Like Togo, which conducts a large smuggling trade with next-door Ghana, the Congo-Brazzaville tries to offset a chronic trade deficit by marketing contraband diamonds from Congo-Kinshasa.

Guinea lives on great expectations. It is one of the world's largest sources of bauxite and has top-grade iron ore, but has not realized the potential of either. Much of this is due to President Sékou Touré's cautious resistance to foreign investment and aid which he fears will compromise Guinea's independence. Still, the possibilities are there.

By contrast, the four giants of the Sahara—Chad, Niger, Mali, and Mauritania—are mostly wastelands of sand and scrub. Together the four contain nearly 2 million square miles, which is all the United States west of the Mississippi, excepting Texas. Yet they can barely support 10 million people, the population of Ohio, among them. All but Mauritania are landlocked, all are predominantly Moslem, all live by subsistence farming or herding livestock on the tiny percentages of their vast areas that have water. Mauritania has hopes that copper and iron-ore deposits will enrich its meager economy. Niger has uranium and untapped iron. Mali and Chad have no miracles to look forward to.

In Moorish Mauritania three-quarters of the people still live in tents, and even sophisticated government officials delight in returning to the dunes for family picnics, drinking mint tea and eating roast goat in nomad tents—while birds die in the trees from heat exhaustion.

In Chad—the French spell it Tchad—transport is by camel or by air. There are no railroads, few miles of all-weather road, and a river navigable only in the rainy season. This is also the time when shallow Lake Chad, one of the country's few sources of water, swells to twice its normal size. The Moslem North is in rebellion against the black, animist South, which is in power.

In Mali, on the bank of the great river Niger, is the once-fabled metropolis of Timbuktu. Now a dusty, sun-baked remnant containing five thousand people, it was once the jewel of the old kingdom of Mali, a center of scholarship and trade, where caravans bearing gold and slaves passed its mosques and mansions.

Such countries are heavily dependent on French aid, and those which have tried to go their own way, like Mali and Guinea, have found economic development extremely difficult. Mali, for instance, chose socialism and independence in 1960, and has stagnated since. Socialism in Africa—it is also a way of life in Kenya, Tanzania (Tanganyika plus Zanzibar, on the east coast), and other African states—is essentially applied to agriculture, where it is hoped that collectivization and communal co-operation will expand output and increase farmers' income, share and share alike. Industry is developed more gradually. In Mali, despite the help of Chinese communist technicians and aid from the Soviet Union and eastern Europe, the program faltered, the government was overthrown, and the pace of socialism has since slackened. But Mali's dismaying economic problems remain. It has Africa's lowest rate of growth and lowest income per head, an estimated $53 per year. Its currency is the most devalued in French Africa. Its five-year plans have been revised, revised again, and then dropped entirely. It spends twice as much on imports as it exports and runs a constant balance-of-trade deficit. The condition became so bad in 1969 that Mali was forced to go, cap in hand, to France and ask that the Mali franc be made convertible and that outstanding debts be paid in return for total French control of the currency.

Half of the heads of state who led the French African countries at the time of independence are still in power, and almost all their countries are on the list of those which have had moderate economic success. *Coups* have occurred as readily in militant as in conservative states, among friends of France as well as among friends of communist China. Almost every *coup* in Africa has been inspired by the army, the only independent power group in the tightly controlled, one-party states. The soldiers seize power, determined to tackle the eco-nomic mismanagement and corruption, only to dis-cover they have underestimated the economic prob-lems. Though some politicians are often corrupt and incompetent, their failure is often due to their coun-tries being too poor and too small to become viable. Even when the soldiers manage to clean up the mess and want to hand over to a civilian regime, they find themselves in Oliver Cromwell's predicament be-cause there is no one else who can do the job so well. And they find themselves saddled with political lead-ership for which they have had no training. The fact that they are in power is no guarantee that other, younger soldiers will not grow dissatisfied at the same lack of national success, and rise to strike them down in their turn.

Future trouble is likely to come in those territories where the economic per-formance is most out of touch with the natural aspira-tions of the people. It is not just a question of sheer poverty. Even some of the poorest countries, such as Niger, have been able to enjoy a comparatively troublefree ride. But in those countries all over Africa where most children go to primary school and can-not find employment when they leave, the seeds of discontent grow fast. If, in addition to this, the civil service and the elite skim off most of the available wealth, the stage is set for the next *coup*. In the sev-enties, any independent or even "semi-free" African country with intractable economic problems—per-manent deficits, unviable markets, and insufficient foreign aid—must run into rough waters.

5 CONGO-KINSHASA

LIGHT IN THE DARK HEART

the silence of the land went home to one's very heart—its mystery, its greatness, the amazing reality of its concealed life. . . . The great wall of vegetation, an exuberant and tangled mass of trunks, branches, leaves, boughs, festoons, motionless in the moonlight. . . . The immense matted jungle with the blazing little ball of the sun hanging over it. The air was warm, thick, heavy, sluggish. There was no joy in the brilliance of the sunshine. . . . Trees, trees, millions of trees, massive, immense, running up high; and at their foot, hugging the bank against the stream, crept the little begrimed steamboat, like a sluggish beetle crawling on the floor of a lofty portico. As we struggled round a bend, there would be a glimpse of rush walls, of peaked grass roofs, a burst of yells, a whirl of black limbs, a mass of hands clapping, of feet stamping, of bodies swaying, of eyes rolling, under the droop of heavy and motionless foliage. . . . Sometimes the roll of drums behind the curtain of trees would run up the river and remain sustained faintly, as if hovering in the air high above our heads, till the first break of day. Whether it meant war, peace, or prayer we could not tell. . . . We were wanderers on prehistoric earth, on an earth that wore the aspect of an unknown planet." *

Such was Joseph Conrad's Congo nearly a century ago, and to a considerable degree it is still unchanged. The hinterland remains a "heart of darkness," a green, humid wilderness, brooding, dank, and savage. Conrad's hippos and crocodiles (he called them "alligators") still bask

* *The Heart of Darkness,* by Joseph Conrad. By permission of Dent, London, and Trustees of the Joseph Conrad Estate.

side by side on "silvery sandbanks"; gorilla families survive in the bamboo forests, and the lush tangles of vegetation on river islands where ancient monsters roamed look much as they did at the dawn of time. Daubed with yellow mud, the grandsons of the cannibals with whom Conrad rubbed shoulders still stalk beneath drab-green domes of fleshy leaves. Rainbows arch the waterfalls and boiling rapids as they always have, and naked, thigh-high pygmies still hunt elephant with tiny bows and deadly arrows.

Yet overall the Congo is groping its way into modern times after a violent and somber history, and has entered an era of relative stability and prosperity. Now the independent Democratic Republic of the Congo—also known as Congo-Kinshasa—it is a great sweltering land mass of 905,382 square miles, larger than Texas and Alaska combined, with a black population of some 18 to 20 million people belonging to more than two hundred tribes. (Europeans number about 113,000.) The equator cuts across the upper third of the country. Nine other African nations almost, but not quite, surround it; a finger of land accompanying the Congo river to the sea gives access to the Atlantic in the west. It is endowed with incredible mineral riches. Currently it is the world's foremost producer of industrial diamonds and cobalt, the free world's fourth most important producer of copper and tin. Some 70 percent of the Congo's export earnings are derived from the sale of copper from the flourishing mines of the province of Katanga. Local industries produce beer and soft drinks, processed foods, textiles, cigarettes, shoes, paper products, glass bottles, gas stoves, transistor radios, chemical products, motor scooters, bicycles, batteries, and construction materials. Fifty percent of the Congo's land area is forested, and millions of dollars' worth of timber is exported annually.

Most of that Congolese secondary industry is geared for export and, in turn, is largely dependent on imports of factory equipment. Principal Congolese exports, apart from minerals are palm oil, rubber, tea, and coffee. With Belgium as the chief supplier, its main imports are vehicles, electrical machinery, rolling stock, petroleum products, cotton, flour, meat, dairy products, and pharmaceuticals. America sends transport equipment, machinery, and cereals to the Congo, and imports palm kernel oil, cobalt, zinc, manganese, and rubber.

In a microcosm of the new, *commercial* rush in Africa, American, Belgian, British, French, Japanese, German, and Italian big businesses are continuing to prospect and develop the Congo-Kinshasa in force, particularly its rich new copper fields. In 1970 its foreign exchange reserves were about $250 million and the national income was being increased at an average rate of 7 percent a year. Its financial condition—helped by $500 million in American economic, military, and development aid —was sound. The Congo had become the first independent African state with resources sufficient to qualify for the inner circle of the International Mone-

tary Fund, a pool of credit subscribed by some one hundred member nations. She took her seat in *Le Club des Dix*, as the IMF elite is known, among some of the richest countries in the world. And it was a black man, a Congolese, in that seat.

Times had changed; remarkably so. From 1885 to 1908, the country had been the personal empire and vast commercial monopoly of King Leopold II of Belgium, whose sharp eye for profit started the European scramble for dominion in Africa. Leopold hired Henry Morton Stanley, who was world-famous for his feat in finding David Livingstone, to explore the Congo and was impressed with the expedition's findings. In 1884 a conference of colonial powers in Berlin had granted Leopold's claim to the territory, which Stanley already had buttressed with a sheaf of treaties arranged with Congo chieftains. The atrocities subsequently inflicted on hapless tribespeople by the white agents of Leopold's concessionaire companies and their barbarous bands of private troops almost beggar description. Where revenue failed to exceed basic expenditure, cruel quotas were set. African workers who failed to bring in the required amounts of rubber, palm oil, or ivory to swell the royal coffers in Brussels were shot out of hand or mutilated. Hands, feet, or ears—and sometimes all three—were hacked off. It is estimated that Leopold's reign over the bizarrely named Congo Free State cost between 5 and 8 million Congolese lives.

Appalled international opinion finally forced the king to relinquish his

115

blood-soaked fiefdom, and from 1908 until independence in 1960 the Congo was governed by Belgium as a colony. For that half century the Congo was Belgium's "silent empire." The torture ceased, but forced labor was quietly continued and strict, paternalistic control was maintained over all aspects of life. The black masses saw little of the vast profits accruing from minerals—including the uranium that went into the atom bomb dropped on Hiroshima. No black was given any post of power in government or commerce. The doors to radical or other dangerous thinking were kept locked.

All political activities by Congolese were rigorously suppressed until the mid-fifties, when the Belgians saw that the Congo's neighbors were fretting on the threshold of freedom. Slowly the Congolese leaders—chiefly a bony, goatee-bearded, spellbinding postal clerk named Patrice Lumumba, who commanded the broadest base of popular support—stepped up demands for independence. Slowly the Belgians gave ground, slowly they introduced reforms.

At the beginning of 1960, after riots by politically agitated mobs were ruthlessly put down, the Belgian government agreed to end the strife and give the Congo its independence. The Belgians figured they would be able to run the country from behind the scenes, while continuing to pocket dividends through their deeply rooted cartels.

The Congolese, having served so long as a labor force for the Belgians, were totally unprepared for freedom when it came. There were no African doctors or attorneys, there was but one black engineer, and only a dozen graduates out of the small number of students at Lovanium University, outside the capital city of Leopoldville (today Kinshasa). In a population then estimated at 15 million, there were fewer than 25,000 Congolese with any kind of training above the primary level.

If the Belgians laid the groundwork for the grave trouble which followed independence, some malign African politicians made certain it would erupt by promising the people—simple and sorely exploited by the colonialists—that the day of liberty would mean the end of all their difficulties. Voters were assured that the homes, the wealth, the wives, and the cars and refrigerators of the white men would be given over to them. Half a dozen black janitors in a Leopoldville brewery firmly believed they would become directors overnight. Some candidates went further, promising their constituents that at the moment of independence their skins would turn white!

On June 30, 1960, under a cloudless azure sky which gave no hint of the carnage to come, the Belgians handed over the articles of independence to portly President Joseph Kasavubu, a former petty *fonctionaire* turned revolutionary, and to the charismatic Lumumba, who had been appointed Prime Minister. In their politicking, Kasavubu and Lumumba shrewdly and effectively evoked the romantic and stirring era of the "true" Congo which flourished long before colonial times. Lumumba based his appeal for a new nationalism on the Congo's old glories, while Kasavubu, a Bakongo, stood before the voters as a descendant of the Bantu hunters and warriors who founded the Kongo Kingdom, one of the largest and most prosperous black states south of the Sahara, around 1400. A typical Sudanic nation of the time, the Kongo Kingdom and its surrounding cluster of smaller states was estimated by a seventeenth-century missionary to have a population of 2.5 million. An engraving of 1642 shows the Kongo king as a handsome and regal figure, attired in silken garments and seated under a chandelier of candles, with the members of a Dutch trade delegation paying tribute at his feet.

Fiery and embittered, Lumumba reflected the mood of his people and lost no time in flaying the former overlords on liberation day. Before a multitude of Congolese chanting "Independence—cha, cha, cha" he delivered a polemic against Belgium and young King Baudouin, who sat glowering at his side on the ceremonial platform. "Who can forget the hangings and the shootings in which so many of our brethren perished?" Lumumba cried. "We have experienced contempt, insults, and blows. We knew the law was never the same for whites and blacks."

Later that day a strapping Congolese warrior ran alongside the royal car, snatched Baudouin's sword from his lap and waved it aloft as a symbol that the bonds of colonialism had been broken. But ahead, lay a holocaust of revolt, civil war, massacres, and political assassinations in which perhaps a million people were to die; for five years the Congo was to be a battlefield on which the major powers of the world fought for influence in free Africa.

The black rank-and-file of the Congo's 25,000-man army, the Belgian-organized but subsequently undisciplined *Force Publique,* had been given to understand that Lumumba would promote them all to sergeants and corporals within hours of independence. When this did not happen and they found themselves still under the orders of white men, the soldiers went beserk, murdering, pillaging, and raping both whites and fellow Congolese. Old tribal antagonisms flared and anarchy loomed. The Belgian troops available were unable to check the uprising, and Kasavubu and Lumumba called in a mixed United Nations force.

In July, Moise Kapenda Tshombe announced the secession of the copper-rich province of Katanga, the mainspring of the Congo economy. It was to be an independent republic with himself as president. Urbane, wealthy, related to one of the tribal royal houses, Tshombe was a right-wing politician widely known to be in league with the Belgians. He was a founder and leader of the powerful CONAKAT party (*Confédération des Associations du Katanga*), which was openly supported by the Belgian government and Brussels mining interests.

The Congo upheaval now

became civil war. In Leopoldville, President Kasavubu quarreled with the radical Lumumba and fired him. The Prime Minister refused to quit and was arrested. Four months later, after an abortive effort to escape, Lumumba was handed over to his archenemies, Tshombe and his black and Belgian allies in Elizabethville (now Lubumbashi), the capital of breakaway Katanga. Soon after his arrival, battered and dazed, in an airliner from Leopoldville, Lumumba was murdered—shot as he knelt, it was said, in the garden of a suburban villa. His death immediately elevated him to martyrdom in the black struggle against neocolonialism.

Ground and air attacks by United Nations forces on Tshombe's well-equipped, 12,000-man Katangese army—stiffened by white mercenaries from Europe, South Africa, and Rhodesia—were launched throughout the fall of 1961 and ended in December with the streets of Elizabethville littered with corpses. But it was not until the middle of 1963 that the Katanga rebellion was finally quelled by force of arms. Tshombe fled to Europe, and the United Nations enforced an uneasy peace on the Congo.

Yet when the UN eventually withdrew, Kasavubu faced a series of uprisings by ambitious men which plunged the nation back into turmoil. Some were simple grabs for power, others expressions of tribal discontent and the economic imbalance among the various sections of the country. The president's fantastic remedy—setting a thief to catch a bunch of thieves—was to call back the arch-

rebel Tshombe from exile and make him Prime Minister of the Congo Republic in hopes that the country's factions could rally around him.

Neither Kasavubu nor Tshombe was able to earn the confidence of his countrymen. In 1965 both were swept away in a bloodless *coup* by the commander of the army, General Joseph-Désiré Mobutu, a powerful, balding ex-sergeant, who had once before seized power during a falling out between Kasavubu and Lumumba. Tshombe again fled. (By 1970 both he and Kasavubu had died.)

Gradually, and with a firmness that often has amounted to ruthlessness, General Mobutu has brought order to the Congo. No human obstacles have been allowed to block the tasks of reconstruction. The number of Congolese provinces has been reduced from an unwieldy twenty-one to eight, thereby streamlining administration and strengthening Kinshasa's control. All the principal tribes are represented at Cabinet and burgomaster levels, a move that has increased, not lessened, national unity. Unity also has been sedulously pursued by Mobutu himself. As leader of the Congo's only political party, the People's Revolutionary Movement, he has regular private talks with representatives of various sections of the community—trade unionists, civil servants, churchmen, journalists, professional and business men, academic leaders, and army and police chiefs—to hear their views on how government might be strengthened and improved. Mobutu's ene-

121

Livestock graze on hillock in typically rolling Congo landscape. Below: Picking ripe tea leaves on plantation. Bottom: Pounding manioc root. Balegas are only Congo tribe that does this chore with musical rhythm. Manioc (or arrowroot) plant was an import from South America.

123

mies (outside the country; no opposition is heard inside) call him a "neocolonialist at heart," a cynic paying no more than lip service to the principles of the martyred Lumumba (whose portrait now adorns a Congolese banknote). But Mobutu denies the charges. He considers himself a "grand chief" who wields his rod for the good of all. This is a traditional and meaningful African concept, and despite the overtones of dictatorship Mobutu's methods appear to be giving the Congo a viable political structure. According to Basil Davidson, the most convincing token of the vision of unity is "the astonishing persistence of the idea of a Congolese nation in the face of every obstacle and provocation to the contrary."

The principal obstacles are unemployment and ethnic rivalries unalleviated by any strong lines of communication, but both are gradually being overcome.

In the struggle, the Kinshasa regime has much on its side and to its credit. A monetary system that was once gravely sick (the Congo was on the verge of bankruptcy at the end of the civil wars and its currency was contemptuously called "Mickey Mouse money") has been robustly rehabilitated with the help of the International Monetary Fund. Electric power and industry are being developed by a $70 million dam complex which has harnessed the mighty Congo river at Inga, between Kinshasa and the estuary port of Matadi.

Economically, Mobutu practices "African socialism," a notably elastic philosophy which encourages private investment on the one hand while nationalizing industries on the other. (Jomo Kenyatta defines African socialism, of which he is a leading proponent, as a "political and economic system that is positively African, not being imported from any country or being a blueprint of any foreign ideology, but capable of incorporating useful and compatible techniques from whatever source.") Those sources include capitalism.

Nationalization of the Congo's big mining and oil corporations, banks, and other major concerns has been highly profitable to the government. The Congolese administration set a record in Africa for this practice when, in January, 1967, a state company named Gecomin expropriated the $1 billion in assets of Union Minière, the giant Belgian copper company, which had held monopoly rights in Katanga.

The government has built a tough, loyal army—the *Armée Nationale Congolaise* —of some 38,000 officers and men drawn from all parts of the Congo. The army, which is the key to power, enforces security—sometimes brutally in dealing with pockets of suspected enemies of the state— in conjunction with the *gendarmerie*, another agency General Mobutu has brought under tight control. Tactical military training has been supplied by Belgium. Israel has trained the companies of paratroopers based in Kinshasa and Katanga, and Italy has molded the Congolese Air Force, which has American fighter and transport planes. The United States has supplied logistical support, ammunition, and more than two thousand vehicles.

The lack of communications and transport networks, which affects the political and social unity of the people, is being tackled resolutely. There are about 100,000 miles of roads in the Congo, but many in the rainy season are treacherous muddy tracks, and rural regions are isolated from each other for weeks on end. But new sections are being added regularly to the 2,000 miles of road already asphalted. Bridges supplied by America, Britain, and West Germany have been set across rivers to replace those destroyed by military action.

There are telephones in all the cities and towns, although many of the latter are little more than a collection of tin roofs. The system is being expanded.

The national airline and several charter companies (which in addition to conventional light aircraft have helicopters for mineral surveys and bush ambulance work) link all the urban and many of the rural areas.

At present there are only some 3,000 miles of railroad throughout the country, and Katanga's mineral wealth is either served by the Benguela railway through Angola (where it is subject to attacks by anti-Portuguese guerrillas) to the coast, or by a series of rail and barge transhipments to Matadi. The government's biggest transport plan is to build a 550-mile trans-Congo railroad linking Katanga with Matadi.

The Congo has 9,000 miles of navigable waterways. Sixteen hundred of these belong to the 2,718-mile-long Congo river, one of the world's largest and longest, and the republic's main highway of leisurely trade. Formed by the confluence of the Luapula and the Lualaba rivers in northern Katanga, it dominates the lives and sets the pace of existence of most of the Congo-Kinshasa's inhabitants. They call it simply "the river"—the male and female workers in the coffee, palm, and rubber plantations along its banks, the store-owners and small businessmen in the riverside communities, the fishermen who brave the rapids to cast their large conical traps, and the stevedores aboard the ocean-going freighters which make the eighty-three-mile journey from the river's wide, muddy mouth to Matadi. Joseph Conrad saw the river, which Stanley followed from the interior to the Atlantic, as "an immense snake uncoiled, with its head in the sea, its body at rest curving afar over a vast country, and its tail lost in the depths of the land." In the lusty ivory-trading days of the Congo river, the seafaring author commanded one of its sternwheel steamers, a "splashing, thumping, fierce river-demon beating the water with its terrible tail and breathing black smoke into the air." Surrounded by barges and bulging with passengers and goods, Mississippi-style steamers still make regular five-day trips between Kisangani (formerly Stanleyville), in the north, and Kinshasa. For thousands of Congolese the steamers are the only link with the world beyond their villages.

Congo at work. Rich copper ore from strip mine (opposite) has been separated from rubble by water under high pressure, is now shoveled onto moving belt. Below: Maintenance-of-way gang. Bottom: Riveter repairs Congo steamer at shipyard in Stanley Pool, the harbor of Kinshasa.

Kisangani is a small graceful town with palm-lined streets, some modern buildings, and an air of lively independence. The scene of bloody battles during the Congo's civil strife, it has returned to its steamy torpor. The lifeblood of Kisangani comes from the river, and on the days that a steamer is due to leave the port the shipping offices teem with activity. Dense, colorful crowds mill about the landing stage. Most passengers arrive long before the scheduled departure time, for there are no reservations on the covers of the "third class" cargo barges attached to the steamer.

After several warning hoots from the steamer's siren, deafening jazz music bursts from a loudspeaker and the vessel leaves amid lusty cheers and farewells. Then one floats, suspended in space and time, it seems, until the next river station is reached and the noise and the chaos begin again. The steamer stops briefly at villages and for an hour or two at river towns like Mbandaka, where it is deathly hot by eight in the morning.

Throughout the day, the steamer glides by brown and green islands dotted with the palm-leaf huts of fishermen. It fusses and dodges through a riot of dazzling tropical color. Crowding either bank are scarlet poinsettia blooms, huge trees overgrown with foliage and creepers, milk-white lilies, and bushes with bright yellow and sky-blue blossoms. At night swarms of fireflies vie with the Milky Way.

Passengers, coming and going at every stop, include Asian traders taking sugar and cigarettes off the boat into remote areas where they will fetch high prices; coal-black provincial officials and dapper, resplendently uniformed army officers on vague missions; tribesmen carrying long poles strung with dried *tilapia*, a nutty-tasting fish of the bream family, and groups of statuesque Congolese women carrying liquid-eyed babies on their backs and reed baskets of rice and spices on their heads.

As the steamer turns southwest toward the sea and the Congo river is joined by the Ubangi, the personality of the waterway changes. Its depths are less black, its banks gentler and more remote. On the northern shore distant hills of an even green replace the dense lines of trees. The river widens, and flows faster to meet the sea. The river traffic changes, too. All along the broad stream, as soon as they sight the steamer and her brood of barges, fishermen and their women put out from the banks in *pirogues*, canoes carved from a single tree.

Sometimes the *pirogues* bring more passengers out from the shores. Always they come to trade. They bring bunches of bananas, or catfish—giant, whiskered specimens up to four and five feet long, flat-headed and menacing in appearance. Some canoes carry even more vicious-looking crocodiles, firmly tied with creepers and with sticks between their jaws. Some are ten to twelve feet in length. They are destined for Kinshasa, where they command high prices from traders who need the belly skins for women's handbags and shoes. In ex-

Train of barges, some carrying cargo, others providing cabins for passengers, makes ten-day round-trip between Kinshasa and Kisangani. Power unit is white ship pushing train (far right). Right: Women on deck; fish for trading. Bottom: Miscellaneous life aboard a passenger barge.

change for the fish and crocodiles, the *commerçants,* mostly women traders who travel on the steamers solely for business, will give lengths of cloth with bright patterns, long, French-type loaves of bread, glass beads and trinkets, vegetables, and other kinds of goods, including canned meat. Money also changes hands, in grubby wads and with hysterical haggling.

Despite all the casual talk of vessels that have sunk during the river voyage or been grounded for days on the sand, the steamer usually arrives in Kinshasa more or less on time. The passengers swarm ashore, the cargoes are unloaded, the decks and cabins scrubbed. It is the end of yet another trip; but the Congo river, stupendous and starkly beautiful, flows on majestically to meet the turquoise deep of the ocean.

With an area of 232 square miles, Kinshasa is one of the largest cities in Africa. Its postindependence name is derived from that of a small fishing village which is now part of the city. Clumps of pale blue and white hyacinths drift past the landing stage of the ferryboat which links Kinshasa with the Congo-Brazzaville, the former French Congo, a small but contentious neighbor whose communist tendencies have led to frequent bitter quarrels (and then to theatrical mid-river reconciliations aboard a ferryboat) with the western-oriented Republic. The story goes that the hyacinths were brought to the Congo many years ago by the wife of a missionary who carried them to her husband's post up-country and planted them in her garden. But instead of remaining there to remind the church-

man's wife of home and civilization, they broke their bonds and crept into the bush and the river. Now the hyacinths choke the tributaries of the Congo river, and when it rises in flood and dislodges them they slip into the muddy yellow-brown current and float with it toward Kinshasa.

Like the hyacinths are the *jeunesse* (youth) of Kinshasa, who have been drawn from up-river villages to the capital. These are the Congolese teenagers who were in school at the time of independence, the children of parents who have lived most of their lives under colonial rule and, like half the country's population, remain rooted in the bush.

Answering some compulsive siren call, the *jeunesse* have bobbed on the surface of a social current and found themselves in a city as brash and thrusting as themselves. They are the new rebels—rebels, they say, against tribal conservatism and the slow, hoary ways of life. They complain that the old are tied to traditions with which they would also tether the young. The *jeunesse* of Kinshasa and other urban centers of the Congo accuse their elders of sustaining the tribal hatreds which have led to bloodshed and misery throughout the land. Like youth elsewhere, they are bewildered, yet militantly impatient for change.

It was the *jeunesse*, in tight trousers, sandals, and shirts unbuttoned to the waist, who stormed foreign embassies in the days of unrest, set ablaze the books in public libraries, and carried through the streets angry placards and effi-

gies, which they later burned, of public figures who had been banished to the political wilderness.

Kinshasa had 400,000 inhabitants in 1960. After the end of colonial tutelage, the rule restricting movements of blacks from the bush to the towns (where they lived under a 9 P.M. curfew) fell into disuse. The resulting unchecked urban influx has swollen the African townships and compounds of Kinshasa to a point where the residents cannot yet be fully absorbed into the commercial and industrial life of the capital. Sixty-one percent of its one million population is made up of persons under twenty years. But few people worry about swollen populations. The president frowns on birth control, and the general attitude is: "The greater the numbers, the greater the nation."

A tour of Kinshasa in an old, garishly painted cab takes the visitor first to the top of a hill named after Stanley. From there the attractive capital is spread at one's feet and the wharves, the steamers, skyscrapers, cranes, and cars and trucks are reduced to toys.

There is a visit to Kinshasa's airport, which has one of the longest runways in the world, and on the return journey a stop at the city's imposing Roman Catholic cathedral. One half of the Congo is Christian, heavily Catholic, while the rest, including a Moslem minority, follow traditional faiths. The Catholics claim to have six thousand priests and nuns working there; some missionaries still operate on foot with native bearers, as in the old hunting-safari days. To some extent, Christianity is being "Africanized," which is to say that African cultural idioms, such as contemporary African music, are now considered compatible with Catholic liturgy and worship of the Christian deity.

During the trip, the cab is stopped by soldiers and police at one of Kinshasa's roadblocks, ostensibly set up to check citizens' identity papers. The other reason for the holdup is precisely that: varying sums of money are extorted from motorists, truck drivers, and pedestrians alike with the cynical, but courteous, demand in the vernacular, *Madesu ya bans* ("Beans for the children"). Such official banditry, whispers the cab driver in French, extends up to Cabinet level.

The cab drives on down a long boulevard lined with well-stocked department stores and high office-cum-apartment blocks to the big central square where, in June, 1966, four of the government's political opponents, including a former prime minister, were publicly hanged after a bizarre, hurried trial. The driver recalls the white coffins that stood open at the foot of the gallows as the victims were led, blindfolded and gagged, to the steps.

"It was a sad sight, *monsieur*," the cabbie says, "but traitors have to die. Our government has to be constantly on guard against subversion; and there are many foreigners who would like to control us—the Belgians, the Americans, the Portuguese, and the Chinese and the Russians in Brazzaville over there."

136

Like most of that hardy breed, the man in the street, he is unsophisticated and notoriously ill-informed. Yet his comments convey an oblique, astigmatic vision of contemporary Congo truths: the commercial Belgians *are* again present in large numbers; suspicion *is* deep-rooted that American aid is a surreptitious effort to buy up the country; the Portuguese *are* eyed with bitter hostility for their repression of black men in neighboring Angola; the Chinese and the Russians *are* actively in evidence; and there *is* uneasiness over the intermittent sabre-rattling of Congo-Brazzaville.

The tour comes to an end at one of Kinshasa's sidewalk cafes, which were introduced by the early Belgian settlers. Congolese civil servants and businessmen mingle with white visitors sipping absinthe as the sun sinks in a mauve-and-rose equatorial sky and throws the tall, twisted palms marching down the promenades into sharp relief. A light evening breeze tempers the stifling heat and humidity. On the opposite side of the street, a red and white candy-stripe awning marks one of Kinshasa's excellent continental restaurants, where imported oysters are served as a prelude to tender steaks with green salads and vintage French wines. Some of these excellent restaurants feature *moamba*, the Congolese national dish consisting of chicken and manioc with hot and spicy palm oil or with peanut sauce on rice.

Kinshasa, like others in Africa, is a schizophrenic city. Herds of goats tended by swathed, wraith-like figures stumble over the cobblestones at night as the distant beat of the tom-toms grows frenzied. But elsewhere there are black-tie symphony concerts; hotels with TV sets featuring American programs in every room; genteel exhibitions of exquisitely wrought Congolese arts and crafts, and nightclubs with spectacular, sophisticated entertainment.

Kinshasa has a new, all-pervading air of well-being, and the future of its *jeunesse* is not all that bleak. Aided by various foreign agencies, the young Congolese are being given ever-increasing opportunities to train as doctors, central and local government officials, journalists, teachers, and the like. The desperate need for education and a literate citizenry is being met by the government as a priority measure. In 1970, ten thousand Congolese were taking college level courses.

With the slogan "Neither capitalism nor socialism, but Congo nationalism," the government is pledged to eradicate the evils of power-grabbing, tribalism, and corruption which brought the country to her knees. It has lived down much of its grim reputation for wholesale horror, and possesses a soundness and strength it has never had before. When King Baudouin returned to the Congo-Kinshasa to join the celebration of its tenth anniversary of independence, Mobutu proudly impressed upon him the importance of the country to the well-being of the entire continent. "When the heart of Africa is ailing," he said, "the rest of the body suffers. But the heart has resumed its normal beat."

6 PORTUGUESE AFRICA

IVILIZATION—AT GUNPOINT

angola, on the southwestern coast of Africa, and Mozambique, on the Indian Ocean in the east, are not colonies of Portugal but "overseas provinces," integral parts of the mother country. Every last one of Angola's 5.5 million inhabitants, and Mozambique's 7 million, is a citizen or ward of Portugal. The Portuguese say that the prolonged strife with the black majorities of their African possessions should be viewed not in the "distorted" and ephemeral context of press reports, but as part of something that began centuries ago and must be allowed to continue for centuries to come. It is, they claim, part of a "civilizing mission," the self-same mission that brought them to Africa originally and will not let them leave. "First in, last out," they declare, adding that today the mission is being carried on not for selfish, narrowly nationalistic motives, but on behalf of the entire Christian world. If most of the Christian world outside Portugal disagrees with the Portuguese approach, that is because it has lost its way and become impure. While the Christian world flounders, the selfless, far-sighted Portuguese will act as its defender and continue to guard her old friends against the savage hordes and godless communism.

The argument is put forward seriously and with sincerity, although when maps are produced to demonstrate the strategic importance of Angola and Mozambique (and the little "ink-blot" of Portuguese Guinea) in any future world conflagration, one is tempted to point out that the deployment of ICBM's and nuclear submarines requires different strategies from those for sixteenth-century fleets of sail. For Portugal's day of glory is past; she survives on successes achieved by swashbuckling explorers making the first voyages of discovery. By the time nineteenth-century Africa became the target for the imperial ambitions of European nations, Portugal already had long-established claims to the territories she holds in her grip today.

When Portuguese adventurers discovered the broad estuary of the Congo river in 1482, they made contact with one of the larger black empires of the era south of the Sahara. This was the Kongo Kingdom, whose monarch, the Manikongo, had his capital in what is now northern Angola. One of the more important of the southern areas within the Kongo Kingdom was known as Ndongo—it included most of the central part of modern Angola—and one of the native rulers of the region possessed the hereditary title *Ngola*. It is from this that the province derives its name.

From the end of the fifteenth century until the last quarter of the sixteenth, the Portuguese concentrated their "civilizing" campaign, which was allied to the trade in slaves, ivory, and gold, on the main Kingdom of the Kongo. Surplus clergy were sent from Portugal as missionaries, along with traders and artisans, and a number of African heathens were converted to Christianity. One convert became king in 1491, and a son who was educated in Portugal and received Holy Orders there became the world's first black bishop.

The creation of a Christian serfdom in savage Africa became of less importance and urgency to Portugal than a speeding up of the slave trade, however, and she turned her back on the Kongo throne to focus attention on the coastal strip of what is now mid-Angola. King Sebastian in Lisbon sent a *conquistador*, Paulo Dias de Novas, and an army to the area in galleons. In 1576, Dias made his base at "Loanda," now the capital Luanda, to the south of the Manikongo's seat of power, and from then on, until 1863, when Queen Mary of Portugal abolished the slave trade, Angola was reduced to a shambles by rapacious bands of slave grabbers. Their cruel and vastly profitable operations, involving men, women, and children, were preceded by a century-long war of annihilation by Portuguese forces against the Ngola of Ndongo, during which shiploads of the conquered regularly were sent to Brazil.

The central Kongo Kingdom was also raided for slaves by the Portuguese. After suffering a series of defeats it fell prey to internal rivalries and dissensions which eventually reduced the once-great kingdom to a few villages.

Complete occupation of Angola was not achieved by the Portuguese conquerors-cum-slavers until the nineteenth century. The state-building operation was a slow but relentless process involving constant warfare with, and pacification of, various tribes. Some succumbed to bribery, taking firearms, ammunition, and such luxuries as colored beads and embroidered cloths as payment for slave raids on neighboring tribes, or for slaughtering elephant herds for the tusks.

Effective civilian occupation of Angola began in 1863 with the arrival from Brazil of the first large group of European settlers, people whose descendants still live in the province today. The move was met with fierce resistance by the blacks, and revolts and insurrections have continued to erupt periodically in the century since, all of them ruthlessly suppressed by the Portuguese.

Mozambique's subjugation was easier. The explorations of Africa encouraged by Prince Henry the Navigator in the fifteenth century made their first landfalls on the west coast. Subsequently the route of discovery was southward, around the Cape of Good Hope, and up the east coast, where, in the seventeenth century, Portugal settled the Zambezi area of what is now Mozambique. It was—and is—a hot, unhealthy haunt of the tsetse fly and malarial mosquitoes, but it was on the gold-export route from ancient Zimbabwe and thus worth enduring.

By the end of the nineteenth century, Mozambique's economic growth had lagged far behind that of its neighbors to the south, where climatic conditions were more favorable. A system of development by chartered companies, which had been instituted by the impoverished home government, lasted for several decades, until Lisbon —with improved medical knowledge helping to overcome Mozambique's serious health hazards—decreed the province to be a single entity under its control,

141

En Route: Conductor (opposite) collects tickets from blacks in fourth-class car, police (below) patrol corridors, and soldier (below right) checks identity papers. Troubles in Angola and railroad links with unfriendly neighbors Zambia and the Congo force Portuguese to watch trains and travelers.

and started making it more accessible by improving road, rail, and air communications.

Angola and Mozambique share a number of geographical and physical characteristics—in addition to the quite serious internal difficulties both have experienced. Each province has attractive, palm-lined bays, placid lagoons, and sweeping, silvery beaches. In the cities, both territories have transplanted the sights and sounds of Portugal—crowded sidewalk cafes, guitar bands, jostling, barefoot lottery-ticket sellers, carafes of green wine, and giant, grilled prawns served with peppery *piri-piri* sauce. Mozambique and Angola each are administered by a Portuguese governor. White and black troops—in mottled jungle camouflage battle-dress—are omnipresent, a total of up to 120,000, backed by fighters, bombers, and helicopters.

Surrounded by the Congo-Kinshasa, Zambia, and South-West Africa, Angola (481,350 square miles) is almost as extensive as western Europe and is Portugal's largest overseas province. Much of her terrain, which is rich in minerals, consists of an escarpment rising from the fertile coastal plain to the high central African plateau. A large proportion of the land is covered with the coffee plantations of white settlers. Angola consistently records a favorable balance of payments and is of considerable importance to the metropolitan economy; but her poor sister Mozambique—302,300 square miles, shaped like a blazing torch, and for the most part open and undulating except for hilly, heavy bush

in the north—is continuously engaged in an uphill economic struggle aggravated by the years of internal conflict. Despite tea, sugar, coconut, tobacco, cotton, sisal, and banana plantations, despite coal, asbestos, and bauxite deposits, and dairy and agriculture produce (including heavy cashew-nut crops). Mozambique has frequent trade deficits. In 1969 alone, she was in the red to the extent of $21 million.

Angola and Mozambique have no tribes in common. But in Mozambique the strong, fierce Makonde, who form the backbone of the freedom guerrillas there, also inhabit the southern half of Tanzania, where they are renowned as sculptors of ebony wood. The Tongas of Mozambique are also to be found in Zambia and Rhodesia, while the *nyanja*-speaking blacks of the province have close relatives who were among the early inhabitants of what are now Malawi and Zambia. In Angola's south there are tribes which extend deeply into South-West Africa, and in the north the Bakongo form the biggest tribe, straddling the Congo-Angola border.

Twenty-three times the size of Portugal, Angola and Mozambique are by any yardstick her most important holdings. They are also her front lines, her most exposed outposts in her self-declared wars against the forces of darkness. Portugal is the weakest and smallest of the old imperial powers. She is also the poorest nation in Europe, but her empire—with the exception of the tiny enclave of Goa—remains as it was at the beginning of the century: Macao, Timor, Cape Verde Islands, Principe and São Tomé Islands (in the Gulf of Guinea, off Gabon), Portuguese Guinea known as Guinea-Bissau, Angola, and Mozambique.

The elements that go into the making of Portugal's experience in Africa are poverty, an unswerving devotion to her cause, and an unwillingness to recognize the advent of the twentieth century. With the support of the whites in power in South Africa and Rhodesia, she continues a bitter struggle against the African fighters sworn to liberate their territories from minority European rule. For Portugal, however, these are not wars of independence, but civil disturbances aided and abetted by her black neighbors in Zambia, Tanzania, and the two Congos, whom she accuses of arming and harboring rebel forces with funds and materials from Russia, mainland China, and Cuba.

Having taken the precaution in 1951 of changing the legal status of her foreign territories from colonies to provinces, Portugal can and does insist that her problems are domestic and thus off limits to interference from the United Nations or any other body or nation. She does not deny that the problems are grave (most of her army is in Africa because of them); she says only that they are her own and no one else's.

This is Portugal's legal position. Her moral position, she says, can be summed up in one word: integration. Portugal does not draw the color line. In theory, the bars of Luanda, the hotels of Mozambique's capital city Lourenço Marques (and white women in both), are as available to the blacks as they are to the whites. All that is asked is that the black man be "civilized," that he speak Portuguese properly, use his knife and fork in the accepted manner, work diligently, practice Christianity, and eschew those heretical dreams of independence. In other words, think Portuguese. In theory, the wonderful world of Portugal is open to anyone —black, white, or mulatto—who seeks it.

In practice, the process of becoming assimilated into the Portuguese culture is a long and difficult one. In practice, it is denied to the great majority of the inhabitants of Angola, Mozambique, and elsewhere; not deliberately, the Portuguese maintain, but because Portugal lacks the funds, and the blacks the skills, for the pace to be any faster. By 1950, when the first stirrings of today's organized, political resistance were felt underground in Angola, less than one percent of the nonwhite population had qualified for citizenship in their own land—this four centuries after Portugal had launched her civilizing mission!

The dream of Portugal is to achieve in her African territories another Brazil, to homogenize the populations, to graft the flower of Portuguese civilization onto the deep, dark roots of Africa. To accomplish this, she requires several centuries of undisturbed labor. The outside world is permitted to help with the financing. But everyone is forbidden to throw rocks at—or in—the greenhouses in which the delicate experiment is taking place.

Tea estate (below) in northern highlands. In background looms Serra Namuli, typical granitic outcrop in this part of Africa. Opposite: Herd of cattle moves through coconut plantation near coastal port town of Quelimane. Tsetse fly and other pests have hurt Mozambique stock raising.

However, Portugal's subjects in Africa and many people in the outside world are not so civilized. Rocks *have* been thrown, much glass has been broken, and gales of change are howling through the greenhouses.

Angola was the first to erupt. There were mass arrests and long terms of imprisonment, with or without trials, for political dissidents in 1924, 1939, and the first half of the fifties. Nevertheless, formation of political parties pledged to ousting the Portuguese began in secret in 1957. There two main movements were the *União das Populacões de Angola* and the *Movimento Popular de Liberacão de Angola*. Their members and leaders were hounded down everywhere by the dictatorship's ruthless secret police.

An African poet, physician, and leading spirit in the new, sophisticated black resistance in Angola, Dr. Agostinho Neto, who had earlier united two main freedom movements under his leadership, was seized in 1960, together with fifty-one other black Angolan revolutionaries. Villagers from Neto's home region east of Luanda who marched in protest against his arrest were massacred by Portuguese troops.

All the signs and portents rightly indicated that Angola's days of peace were numbered. During the same year, the Congo-Kinshasa, which shares an ominously long, 1,300-mile northern frontier with Angola, had been given independence by the Belgians and immediately plunged itself into disaster. Angolan resistance leaders passed back and forth across the frontier with the Congo, which consists mainly of forest, swamp, mountains, and elephant grass, and is easily penetrated. The Portuguese countered an increasing number of African nationalist demands for liberty with greater acts of repression. There were shootings and mysterious disappearances. But strict censorship and the secrecy which by tradition cloaked the efficiently deadly activities of the former state security police, the *Policia Internacional e de Defensa do Estado* (P.I.D.E.), kept the news of disturbances from the majority of the inhabitants. Consequently, the Portuguese settlers believed they were safe. They believed their blacks were happy and would rather be Portuguese than free, and that unpleasant incidents were isolated and unconnected, the work of outside agitators who would speedily be rooted out and liquidated. So, when the first big rocks were hurled in Angola in the early spring of 1961 and landed terrifyingly in the seaport metropolis of Luanda, they caught the Portuguese by surprise. Active revolution had begun.

At night, African crowds stormed the Luanda jail and two police barracks in an unsuccessful effort to free their imprisoned leaders. Seven men were killed, and at their funerals the next day heavy rioting broke out. The army and police, together with armed settlers shouting "animals" at their victims, went on a rampage among the crowded hovels of the capital's African townships. Blacks were shot down and indiscriminately beaten, and there were secret mass burials in the bush of the corpses of African victims.

The brotherhood which was said to veneer relationships between blacks and whites in Angola was stripped away overnight. Offshore Portuguese warships trained their guns on the African slums of Luanda. Armored cars patrolled the streets and soldiers shot to kill. Gangs of Portuguese toughs roamed at will, stoning blacks, lynching them, dismembering them, tossing them from the windows of tall buildings. The police and P.I.D.E. agents executed political prisoners and suspects by the score.

In March, 1961, the Bakongo of the north erupted. It is not clear just what sparked the rebellion, whether it was planned by leaders of an Angolan liberation organization at their headquarters across the border in the former Belgian Congo, or arose spontaneously out of a labor disturbance on one of the northern coffee plantations. But revenge and counterterror were launched by groups of blacks which had gathered in the forests, and the horror spread swiftly. Within the first twenty-four hours, and in forty different locations stretching from Luanda north to the Congo frontier, African revolutionaries invaded the homes and coffee plantations of whites. Between two and three hundred Portuguese were killed, brutally and indiscriminately. Farmers, soldiers, priests, and women and children were sought out and butchered, most of them with spears or knives. The bodies were horribly mutilated. Plantation buildings were burned. In the next few weeks, seven hundred more whites were massacred throughout the upper half of Angola.

Within the first week of the pitiless conflict, Portuguese soldiers moved in and, joined by white vigilante groups from the coffee plantations, began to strike back. They set African villages ablaze with napalm bombs and incendiary bullets. Those inhabitants who did not escape into the bush were slaughtered.

It is still not known just how many Africans were killed, but the figure of seven thousand in the first three weeks of the northern rising is not emphatically denied by the Portuguese authorities. And seven weeks after it began a senior Portuguese army officer in Luanda was quoted as telling newsmen: "I estimate that we have killed thirty thousand of these animals [meaning men, women, and children suspected of working with the the terrorists]. There are probably another hundred thousand, and we intend to wipe them out when the dry season starts."

The Portuguese administration tried to deny that its soldiers had done most of the killing. It suggested that planters and farmers, deranged by the murder of their families, had run amok, severing the heads of many of the blacks they killed and placing them on poles as a warning to rebels. Some Portuguese troops were said to have been sickened by the sight, but the rebel blacks were not inhibited or deterred.

The Angolan rebellion continues, although a certain air of stability has returned to the plantation area. The Africans now working the coffee plantations in Angola—carefully watched by Portuguese overseers carrying rifles—are there on six-month contracts. Most are men, some are women, and a few are boys of twelve and thirteen. Forced labor, a form of paid slavery, has been dropped as a matter of policy by the Portuguese and contract labor substituted. In theory, Africans no longer have to work if they do not wish to, but in practice most work because they must. There are taxes to be paid and, in addition, there is the deeply ingrained Portuguese belief that part of the civilizing mission is to instill in Africans the habit of working for a living. In 1943 one Portuguese colonial minister put it this way: "It is necessary to inspire in the black the idea of work, and of abandoning his depravity, if we want to exercise a colonizing action to protect him. . . . If we want to civilize the native, we must make him adopt as an elementary moral precept the notion that he has no right to live without working."

Since then the Portuguese government has introduced certain reforms to temper the harsh quality of its colonial rule. But the patronizing philosophy remains—and the dedicated opposition to it.

Luanda, Angola's charm-ing, tile-roofed and arcaded center, is remarkable for the absence of a color barrier. Nowhere else in Africa does one see whites and blacks working together, not as boss and hired hand, but as hired hands together. Stevedores at the docks are white and black. In restaurants the busboys are white and black. This unselfconscious mixing of the races has a relaxing effect. One feels that this is the way it was meant to be all along, and what a pity it is mankind did not learn about this sooner. But in Luanda, as elsewhere, appearances are misleading. The influx of poor whites from Portugal in recent years (brought in not only to relieve the unemployment problem in the metropolis, but also to enlarge Portugal's foothold in Africa) has had the effect of squeezing Africans out of jobs. What is more, the white laborer in Luanda tends to receive twice as much pay for the work he performs as does his African counterpart. Outside Luanda, in the hinterland districts, the ratio becomes four or even five times as much. "In the Portuguese African territories the two races have learned to work together, to play together and to live together better than they have at any place on the continent," says a pamphlet distributed by an organization of Portuguese companies that do business in the motherland and its overseas provinces. "The African citizen in Angola and Mozambique has no sense of inferiority, precisely because

Aerial view (below) of Angola's
capital, Luanda, shows old and
new architecture on waterfront
road. Domed building is elderly
bank favored by promenaders for
shady arcade and sidewalk cafes.
Tower bank is recent. Opposite:
Freight yards for Mozambique's
port capital Lourenço Marques.

he is and always has been treated as a member of the human family." In view of Portugal's centuries-long harsh domination in Angola and Mozambique, one is tempted to question the pamphlet's definition of "human family." But what is truly interesting is the pamphlet's implication that there could be and would be no human family in Angola and Mozambique without the Portuguese presence. That incredible document puts it this way: "The lamps of civilization are growing dim in tropical Africa and they may go out entirely if the European is to be excluded from every vestige of political and economic control. . . .

"The mistakes of the past few years should have taught the free world this supreme lesson: without the European, tropical Africa will deteriorate and it might slip back to primitive tribalism. Money alone won't insure progress because no amount of technical advice or technical assistance from outside can get the job done. There is no substitute for the European settler who has made his permanent home in Africa, who knows its problems and who intends to remain there. Without the permanent settler, tropical Africa will be a drain in perpetuity on the resources of the free world while its own resources go undeveloped." *

In other words, although it is claimed that the black man does not feel inferior in Angola and Mozambique, he is inferior by Portuguese definition; if he were not inferior, there would be no need for Portugal's "civilizing" mission in Africa. Thus, while Portugal has officially eliminated the color bar, her colonizers act out of a belief in white supremacy which is almost as devout as that held by the Boers of South Africa and the white Rhodesians. Although *apartheid*, the principle of "separateness," is not Portugal's policy as it is South Africa's, Africans in Angola and Mozambique do in fact live apart. They are separated from the whites in living quarters in both urban and rural areas of the African provinces. When whites are found living among blacks, it is not because they are consciously and willingly practicing integration, but because, in most cases, they are too poor to live elsewhere. When pressed, the Portuguese will admit that the vast bulk of the population is still very African and that the civilizing mission, to effect really profound changes, must by necessity proceed slowly. "You know how Africans really are," they finally say, winking slightly. "They are like little children."

For the Portuguese the living proof of the efficacy of their mission lies in their mulattoes. Here, under this cafe-au-lait skin, is the true essence of multiracialism. There are not many of them (perhaps no more than sixty or seventy thousand in Angola and Mozambique) but they are important because it is so readily apparent that they have assimilated the Portuguese manner. They talk, act, and think like Portuguese; they are civilized. Officially, the Portuguese take pride in their mulattoes, and as a result the mulattoes tend to be better educated and hold better jobs than some of their darker-skinned though equally civilized brethren. But here

* Reports on Portuguese Africa (Race Relations #2). Presented by Overseas Companies of Portugal, Rua do Ataide, 7, Lisbon, Portugal.

again the official policy does not jibe with true feelings. When the revolts broke out in Angola and Mozambique, the groups singled out by the white population and the P.I.D.E. for questioning, imprisonment, or speedy execution were the educated Africans, the leaders, and, of course (because they were rife with education and leadership), the mulattoes. If in those early days after the first bloodshed in Luanda it was dangerous to walk the streets with a dark skin, it was even more dangerous to walk them with a brown skin.

The miscegenation which produced the mulatto population is not the result of official policy. It was practiced haphazardly and casually by Portuguese men who came to Africa without white women. The results of their unions with African women, *mulheres de necessidade*, as they called them, were sanctioned retroactively by church and state, and their offspring became citizens of Portugal. Had the white women continued to stay away from Angola and Mozambique, mixed unions might in time have seriously affected the complexion of these territories. But white peasant women are arriving in increasing numbers and, as they do, the necessity for *mulheres de necessidade* decreases proportionately. But, say the Portuguese, intermarriage is common. One has only to look about. And, just looking about, it does seem to be true. In the cafes, black men sit with mulatto women and in the nightclubs white men dance with black women.

But although some white and black men marry mulatto women in Angola and Mozambique, marriages between black and white are rare. The tendency increasingly is to marry one's own kind. And so the dream of a new Brazil in Africa goes up in smoke.

Is the Portuguese idea of a multiracial community in Africa a total sham? Perhaps the most biased and yet authoritative answer comes not from the Portuguese or even other sources in Angola or Mozambique, but from Dar-es-Salaam in Tanzania. Dar-es-Salaam (the "haven of peace") has become a sanctuary for dozens of African liberation groups and among these is the "Front for the Liberation of Mozambique," better known as Frelimo. The Portuguese, says a Frelimo leader, have no interest in mixing the people. "They are using the multiracial line to hoodwink the world."

Frelimo is the biggest of a number of Mozambique liberation movements. All these groups depend on the support of the countries which provide them with bases out of which they operate: Guinea for Portuguese Guinea; Congo-Brazzaville, Congo-Kinshasa, and Zambia for Angola; Zambia and Tanzania for Mozambique. In the early days—the late fifties and early sixties—they were all made most welcome. Liberation fever was in the air and no self-respecting, newly independent African capital would have considered itself complete without its cluster of freedom fighters from South Africa, the Portuguese territories in Africa, and Rhodesia. Money and arms (from East and West) flowed in as the expatriate leaders vied with each other for still more.

Small landholders (right) work hard with crude tools to raise peanuts. Giant Cassequel plantation (opposite) is corporate farm, has 5,000 workers growing sugar and cotton. Rough terrain limits navigability of rivers, but produces spectacular falls, like Duque de Bragança (below).

Some grew rich at the expense of their followers and, in time, disillusionment set in among some of the host governments. Not only were the liberation wars not being won; they were, in many cases, not even being fought, except in the restaurants and bars of luxury hotels. Furthermore, liberation groups now and again tended to assume they were a law unto themselves, creating disturbances in capitals whose governments were having enough difficulty controlling their own populations.

For all that, it is likely Portugal will be savagely battling guerrillas in her African possessions for many years to come. In Angola the fighting generally takes the form of spasmodic encounters in the north, near the Congo border, between army patrols and bands of rebels. At the end of 1970, a half to two thirds of little Portuguese Guinea had been won by the freedom fighters, and a Portuguese force had deliberately invaded Touré's adjoining Guinea by sea in the hope of toppling him and eliminating leaders of the rebels against Portuguese rule. The invaders failed in both objectives. In Mozambique the Portuguese are facing a tougher challenge from guerrillas, who began operations three years after those in Angola. As in Angola, the problem is one of a long and porous border. The Ruvuma river, a sluggish brown stream inhabited by crocodiles, runs east from Lake Malawi (once Lake Nyasa) to the Indian Ocean. It forms the border with Tanzania, the base of operations for the Mozambique rebellion, and is virtually impossible to effectively police. The insurgents train in camps in Tanzania

155

and in most cases their instructors are Chinese communists. (The Portuguese make much of the fact that the rebels fight with Chinese arms. The rebels and the black, Arab, Asian, and white nations which support them, make an equal fuss over Portuguese use of NATO weapons, and maintain that Lisbon could not carry on the wars without them.)

The rebels slip back and forth across the border with ease, but they operate in barren and desolate terrain, dry bush country unsuitable for cattle because of the tsetse fly. This area (about one-tenth of Mozambique) is of little interest to the Portuguese and they say they have deeded it to the insurgents. But further south, and running parallel with the Ruvuma to the sea, there are two rivers—the Messalu and the Montepuez. Between these two rivers and stretching inland for a distance of about a hundred miles, the Portuguese have applied a scorched-earth policy. At least 250,000 Africans have been moved out of this strip. Some of them unwillingly because this was their home; others went willingly because they feared the rebels. But all of them went and as they departed the Portuguese burned their villages and what remained of their harvest, leaving nothing of any possible use to the guerrillas. The Portuguese patrol this area by plane and on foot. Anything that moves is shot.

The Makonde, who largely fight the fierce guerrilla battles in Mozambique, have faces slashed with tribal scars and their teeth filed to points. Not very long ago they were cannibals. They are excellent fighters, feared and hated by the neighboring tribes. Perhaps it was the activities of the Makonde that led a rival liberation group to accuse them of killing more Africans than Portuguese!

The Africans of Angola and Mozambique are among the most backward of Africa's tribes. Despite centuries of colonial rule, the tribes of the bush do not yet mark the white man as the ultimate enemy. It takes sustained propaganda and a certain sophistication to develop antagonisms drawn along nationalistic rather than tribal lines, so for the time being the Makonde with their cruel ways may remain for some blacks far more frightening than the Portuguese farmer, even when the latter makes his appearance with a weapon in one hand and a six-month labor contract in the other.

Tribal divisions are finely drawn between the Makonde, the Macuas, and the Nhanja of the north, the Sena and Manica in the center, and the Tonga and Changones in the south. Paradoxically, it is the Portuguese language that is the unifying factor among these tribes and little else. This is at once Portugal's strength and her Achilles' heel. The more she educates the people, the more widely used the Portuguese language, the greater the danger of disunited tribes finding common cause with each other against Portugal. But the Portuguese do not believe than any galvanic coalescence of her African populations is imminent. Education is still being handed out parsimoniously; dissident African leaders (Portugal prefers to call them "outside agitators") are being kept out of her territories or jailed when they do appear, and the Portuguese are certain time is on their side and against the Africans.

Already, so the Portuguese argue, "their" Africans see that all has not been well in the so-called independent states. There has been chaos, bloodshed, confusion, and corruption. In fact, everything is worse now than it was before. While the independent black republics slip into anarchy and hopeless poverty, the Portuguese possessions will be moving upward.

Slowly, imperturbably and inefficiently, the Portuguese are struggling to do that. The economies of Angola and Mozambique remain primarily agricultural (as yet only about 5 percent of Angola's arable land is under cultivation), but both are beginning to industrialize and to explore their subsurface wealth. Diamonds are now Angola's second most valuable export and she is developing her iron ore and oil deposits. Mozambique is prospecting for oil, gold, and uranium; and, although harassed by terrorists, she is building a tall, $350 million dam—Cabora-Bassa—across the Zambezi in the south for mammoth hydroelectric and irrigation schemes. The future may look brighter; but, for the Africans at any rate, a boom period will be a long time coming. Because of the continuing guerrilla wars, both Angola and Mozambique are carrying crippling defense burdens. And since the new enterprises are financed and operated by white men, most of the profits will continue to go to them.

The trickle-down theory of economic prosperity cannot have much attraction for the black man of Angola and Mozambique, especially when he realizes that it is his cheap labor that marks the difference between profit and loss. But there is little he can do about it. The Portuguese do not encourage trade-union movements and deplore strikes. The civilizing mission must continue—despite thousands dead and barbarism on both sides.

Portugal's policies appear to have moderated somewhat since the death of the dictatorial Dr. Antonio de Oliveira Salazar. Undoubtedly changes will be made affecting the provinces in Africa. Lisbon has announced that henceforth her overseas territories will be "autonomous within the unitary Portuguese state," yet it is unlikely that the change will be more than semantic. Portugal is not ready to let go of her possessions. Without Angola and Mozambique, she is nothing more than an anachronistic enclave on the Iberian peninsula. If Portugal has done nothing else, she has made certain that her African provinces remain totally unprepared for independence. And it is doubtful whether the rest of the world will force Portugal's hand in the matter of liberation. The memories of the Congo and Nigeria remain too vivid for it to invite further, and perhaps even bloodier and more costly, international adventures in Africa. Meanwhile, Portugal will go ahead, for a few more centuries if necessary, with her sacred mission. Outsiders are asked, politely, to look the other way while she battles to make time stand still.

ADVENTURES IN INDEPENDENCE

ethiopia

ethiopia and Liberia lie on opposite sides of the African continent. Not only is the distance between them immense, but their people do not think alike, talk alike, or even look alike. Ethiopia, most of which is high plateau rising from the Somali desert, is undoubtedly one of the most picturesque countries in all Africa. Within its rugged borders are strangely capped mountains bathed in misty radiance, great patchwork patterns of fields and flowers, valleys deep in shadow, and carpets of searing sand. Liberia is flat, humid, and for the most part—excepting some savannah—densely forested.

Yet Ethiopia and Liberia share common bonds. They are Africa's oldest independent nations and both have close and long-standing ties with America. They are far ahead of other countries in terms of experience, although far behind in terms of accomplishment. In the case of Liberia, the bonds with the United States are deeply historic and fundamental to the divisions which exist between the Americo-Liberians of Monrovia, the capital, and a score of indigenous tribes in the hinterlands. With Ethiopia, the ties are politically related to development, particularly as regards communications.

Largely ignored in the great nineteenth-century European scramble for Africa, and steeped in the past, Ethiopia and Liberia are among the most backward states on the continent. But like a lion loosed in the streets the twentieth century is upon them. Whether they will tame it or be devoured by it is still uncertain.

Ethiopia, dominating the horn of Africa, is the continent's fortress empire. From the oven-hot lowlands bordering the Red Sea, the mountains of Ethiopia rise suddenly like the hackles on a watchdog's back. Range upon range of jagged peaks confound the intruder and barricade the Ethiopians against the rest of the world. The terrain has made the people of Ethiopia what they are— proud, strong, conservative, and suspicious not only of strangers but of each other. The dominant, although not the largest, tribe is the Amhara. The name, derived from Arabic, means "mountain people." Their origins are Semitic and they came as conquerors from Arabia thousands of years ago, seized the peaks and plateaus of the interior and dug in, interbreeding with the original inhabitants, the Hamites. In Greek, the word "Ethiops" means "he of the burnt face," but the Amharas do not believe they are black. And most emphatically they do not believe they are Bantu. As if to make clear the distinction, they made slaves of the Gallas and other tribes that lived within the borders of Ethiopia. The practice has only recently been discontinued.

The Amharas make up about 40 percent of the population. They are an incredibly handsome people. Their bearing is haughty and their skins range in color from light brown to luminescent black. The Gallas, who are divided into many tribes, are the largest group, constituting perhaps half of the population. They are a Nilotic people, quick to fight, hard-working (harder working than the Amharas), and superb horsemen. Their women have the whitest teeth and the loveliest smiles in Africa. The rest of the population is divided among Moslem Somalis, their cousins the Danakils, the Sidamas, and others. Altogether this polyglot population speaks seventy different languages, of which Amharic is the official one. There has never been a complete census but an estimated 23 million people live within this 398,350-square-mile empire.

Although Ethiopia did not achieve political unity until just before the turn of the century, she traces her history and her royal lineage far back in time, back to where truth and legend meet and become one. Thus it is told that centuries ago Ethiopia was ruled from the capital of Axum by a Queen Makeda, otherwise known as the Queen of Sheba. Hearing tales from a traveler, the Queen of Sheba set forth to visit Jerusalem. There she met King Solomon, who converted her to Judaism and sent her back to Ethiopia with child. On the birth of her son, the Queen named him Menelik, and Solomon, hearing the news in far-off Jerusalem, decreed that none but Menelik and his successors should rule over Ethiopia.

The legend is scorned by scholars, but the Ethiopians believe it and, in this respect, what is believed is far more important and relevant than what is true. One does not travel to Axum today in a pedantic search for truth but to revel in mystery. It is said (although not by scholars) that this jumble of stones, this disordered scattering of massive pylons and pedestals, was once the heart of a great empire that stretched over much of eastern Africa and large parts of western Arabia, an empire whose people worshipped the moon, the sky, the sun, the sea, and the earth. If this is not the land of the Queen of Sheba, and these broken stones her capital, then what is?

Axum exudes mystery. Who erected the giant granite columns, some of them taller than the tallest obelisks of Egypt, and carved them to resemble the multistoried earthen skyscrapers of southern Arabia? What tools did the artisans use? How did they hoist the giant steles into position? Who occupied the ancient thrones, and who the cavernous tombs carved out of the nearby hillsides?

Perhaps they were pagan. Perhaps they followed the Hebrew faith or perhaps they were Christian. Here again fact and fancy intermingle. We are told that Christianity was introduced into Ethiopia in 330 A.D. by two shipwrecked Syrian youths, Frumentius and Aedesius. Brought to the court of the king, the two brothers served as tutors to his children and keepers of the royal archives. Over the years, they converted the king and his household to Christianity. Under the authority of the patriarch of Alexandria, Frumentius became the Abuna, or archbishop, of Ethiopia. For 1,600 years the heads of the Ethiopian church were Egyptian Copts, most of whom could neither speak Geez, the language of the Ethiopian priests, nor any of the secular languages. Finally, in 1951, after twenty years of negotiation, Ethiopia won the right to appoint her own Abuna.

Lalibela, north of Addis Ababa, is considered to be Ethiopia's Jerusalem, with eleven churches hewn from solid rock by Copts in 11th-12th centuries. Right: Cruciform structure has top at ground level. Conceived on big scale (below), carved churches each took decades to complete.

Axum lies four hundred miles north of Addis Ababa, Ethiopia's modern-day capital. Between them, at a height of almost two miles above sea level, is the village of Lalibela, Ethiopia's "Jerusalem." There, for reasons best known to themselves, the Coptic priests of the twelfth and early thirteenth centuries caused eleven churches to be built. They were no ordinary churches but were carved into the living rock of the mountainside. Massive and cruciform in shape, their flat roofs are level with the surrounding countryside. In a way, they seem the very essence of Ethiopian Christianity—time-consuming (each took more than thirty years to complete), withdrawn, defensive, and unchanging.

The rituals of Christian worship in Ethiopia are at once colorful and enormously tedious, with bearded priests under multi-hued umbrellas, acolytes with incense, a sing-song litany, tinkling cymbals, and booming drums. Yet for its practitioners it is an exacting religion.

Fasting—in general this means abstaining from such "rich" foods as eggs, meat, and milk—is considered the essence of worship, and the Coptic Christians of Ethiopia fast forty days before Easter, the longest and most important fast of the year. At Christmas there is a voluntary fast of up to a month, and later sixteen fasting days are set aside in remembrance of the Assumption of Mary. Each Wednesday and Friday of every week of the year are also fast days, but only the strictest Coptic worshippers—about 5 percent—confine themselves to the single "meal" of a handful of peas or beans and a glass of water. Failure to observe fasts can result in excommunication. It has been said that fully a third of the Christian population is nominally excommunicated at any given time.

The clergy is numerous and poorly educated. Services are conducted in Geez, which, being a forgotten language, is not understood by the worshippers. Monks and monasteries abound and celibacy is sometimes carried to extremes. On the islands of Lake Tana, for example, the monks have barred all female animals.

If the Coptic church tends to hold Ethiopia back, it also tends to hold Ethiopia together. Although perhaps there are more Moslems and pagans than Christians in Ethiopia, it is the church that sanctifies the continuity of Ethiopia's rulers and it is the church that bridges that otherwise unbelievable gap between truth and legend. Thus the church subscribes wholeheartedly to the doctrine that His Imperial Majesty, Haile Selassie I, King of Kings, Elect of God and Conquering Lion of the Tribe of Judah, is Ethiopia's two hundred and twenty-fifth emperor in the dynasty of Solomon and Sheba. To think otherwise is blasphemous.

If he is not of the seed of Solomon, Haile Selassie at least carries within him all that is required of a true emperor. And if his decisions are not always worthy of Solomon, at least they have the same force and effect as those of the Great King. Indeed, one suspects that his attributes are as much a product of heredity as they are of environment. In the Never-Never Land of Ethiopia Haile Selassie's word is law and neither the steady encroachment of the twentieth century nor the tentative beginnings of parliamentary democracy can alter this simple fact. The emperor himself presides over the advent—marked by widespread American aid in dollars and advisers—of modernity into Ethiopia, letting it in or holding it back as if with sluice gates.

"We must make progress slowly," he has said, "so as to preserve the progress we have already made."

It is the emperor who initiates decisions, both large and small, and those who wish for help, change, justice, or mercy must come to him. There is a period in each of the emperor's working days reserved for the hearing of petitions from his subjects. They approach him bending low, and when the emperor has heard them out and has made his decision, they bend low again and shuffle backwards from the room. No one turns his back on the emperor.

On his frequent tours of Ethiopian provinces Haile Selassie rides in a specially built vehicle, air-conditioned to keep out the dust, and he rides up front on a seat built high so that he will seem taller than his driver. As his vehicle approaches each town, the villagers who have been waiting for him prostrate themselves on the ground, then break through the ranks of police lining the route to cheer, to wave, to touch, to bless, and to present petitions.

The petitions, laboriously lettered in Amharic (the written language contains 276 characters) by village scribes, are rolled up and tied with string. The police try to beat off the petitioners with staves, but still the crowds press forward. Occasionally the emperor may lower his window and receive several petitions with his own hand; but more often equerries gather them up while the monarch, completely unruffled, nods solemnly behind his closed window. He will, in time, reply to each of the petitions, rendering justice meticulously and with awesome finality.

One of Haile Selassie's decisions is often related to illustrate his wisdom. It also illustrates the picayune nature of many of the problems that absorb his day. It seems that a government bureaucrat had paid an Ethiopian girl one Ethiopian dollar (the equivalent of forty cents in the U.S.A.) for a night of her favors. The encounter led to others and, in due course, the bureaucrat married the girl. Years later, however, the gentleman, having risen to ministerial rank, decided that his wife was no longer suitable. He filed for divorce, but refused to split with his wife the $5,000 he had saved during his marriage. The law required that he must, but the minister argued that the money had been accumulated through his efforts and not those of his wife. Eventually (as all things do in Ethiopia) the case came before the emperor who heard the whole story and then mused: "Ten years. That is 3,650 nights. At a dollar a night that would be $3,650." The minister blanched, reconsidered, and decided to stay married.

Danakil nomads (below) inhabit desert area near Red Sea, have a deserved reputation for ferocity. All men carry long-bladed knife as tool and weapon. Meat dries atop hut of plaited grass mats held up by wooden hoops. Opposite: Woman has nose ring and ritual tattoos on cheeks.

To accompany His Imperial Majesty on a trip, to see him in his palace in Addis Ababa, is to be plunged back through the centuries. But which century, and in what land? His ministers wear striped trousers and black frock coats. The emperor himself, a diminutive five feet one inch, but nonetheless a commanding presence, wears an olive-green uniform. On the steps of his palace are two cheetahs. The visitor is urged to stroke their heads. They are said to be drugged to make them calm; but the visitor has not been drugged and is, therefore, not so tranquil as the cheetahs. The palace is quiet, terribly quiet. Footsteps make no sound on the heavy carpets; telephone bells are muted. The emperor himself speaks almost in a whisper but, since there are no other sounds, his voice is heard. When the emperor travels to the provinces, on the other hand, it is like a swirling medieval court. Messengers arrive and depart on horseback or motorcycle, trumpets sound, whistles are blown, commands shouted, salutes exchanged. Guests and camp followers—their petitions ready for presentation at a moment's notice—crowd to eat under tents that have been erected on the hillside, scraping strips of raw beef with their knives from freshly slaughtered carcasses. The emperor emerges from his tent. A group of priests who have been making a din with cymbals and drums is pushed back and told to be quiet by an army officer brandishing a riding crop. The priests cling together like flustered sheep, confused, apprehensive, and out of place, but they make no more noise. The emperor, preceded by a minuscule chihuahua and surrounded by silence, walks past. He steps into his Rolls-Royce limousine. Officers who have whistles blow them and

168

motion frantically and, as the emperor drives off, the priests pick up their drums and cymbals again, while the guests under the tents resume their banquet.

Haile Selassie mounted the throne in 1930. He did not inherit this prize but wrested it from the appointed heir through a skillful *coup d'état.* Six years later he was routed by Mussolini's troops and fled to England, to become the pitied but ignored little figure who pleaded in vain with the League of Nations for collective action against the aggressor. The Italian occupation of Ethiopia came to an end in 1941 (it was the first and last time Ethiopia was colonized by a foreign power), and five years to a day after his departure Haile Selassie returned. The invading Italian armies had used mustard gas on his defenseless population and, during their occupation, had killed thousands more, but Haile Selassie decreed that his subjects should forgive and forget. The time had come to think of the future.

The measurement of progress in Ethiopia is something best avoided by outsiders. The foreign engineer who points out gloomily that there are fewer useable roads in Ethiopia today than there were during the time of the Italians is undoubtedly right, but his view of progress is narrow and specialized. The American Point Four technician who asks you not to mention the fact that the Ethiopians have taken to growing a narcotic leaf called *Khat* on the terraces he has so laboriously built on the precipitous heights leading down from Asmara to Massawa does so because he rightly thinks that other Americans (especially American congressmen) would not understand. The Norwegian naval officer who thinks the Ethiopians will sink their entire navy the day his group of advisers puts them on their own is also taking a parochial view. The disappointments suffered by well-meaning foreign advisers are legion and never ending. Doggedly, Ethiopia remains the land of Evelyn Waugh's *Black Mischief.*

All this is true, but it tells no more about Ethiopia than the face of a clock tells about its inner workings. (Even clocks in Ethiopia may frustrate an outsider seeking to measure progress, for many tell a different time. The Ethiopian day [and clock] begins at dawn—6 A.M. by our manner of reckoning, 12 by theirs. Thus when our watches read 11 A.M., theirs may read 5 A.M. As if this were not enough, there are thirteen months in the Ethiopian calendar—twelve months of thirty days each and an additional thirteenth month of five days, six in leap years. Futhermore, the Ethiopian calendar is seven years behind the Gregorian calendar used by us.) The complicated inner workings of Ethiopia are known perhaps to only one man on earth—Haile Selassie. And what he understands most profoundly is that movement forward must come slowly and from the inside out, not the outside in. Haile Selassie's technique often seems hopelessly Byzantine, but in essence it amounts to a skillful process of giving ground and taking it, of playing one side against the other, of building up and undermining, and all the while making certain that the clock continues to run.

In a certain sense the Italian invasion and occupation played into Haile Selassie's hands. During those five years the irascible *rases,* the warlords and provincial bosses of Ethiopia, had largely been exterminated. Those who remained constituted the chief threat to the emperor. Haile Selassie knew them well, having himself been a *ras* of Harar Province before seizing the throne, and he took the precaution of creating no new ones. The power of those who remained was and is still being whittled down, and the provinces, once the personal fiefdoms of the noble *rases,* have come under the control of the central government. At least in theory there are no more private armies in Ethiopia and the *rases,* their teeth removed, have all they can do to hold on to their vast estates. But these too are being absorbed by Haile Selassie who, in this case, serves as middleman between the owners and the peasants. Land reform is one of the keys to Ethiopia's future, but here again it is being approached slowly, piecemeal, as if in fear that the peasants might choke if fed too much reform at once.

Ethiopia's central plateau is immensely fertile. As yet no one has challenged Mussolini's assertion that Ethiopia, with proper development, could be made to feed half of Europe and all of the Middle East. But even today only about 15 percent of the arable land is farmed. Part of this is the fault of the peasant who, through the centuries, has become convinced that he will be robbed of all surpluses by the nobles whose land he cultivates.

Ethiopia's principal crop is coffee (the province of Kaffa gave birth to its name) and almost three-quarters of the crop reaches the United States. But since it grows wild so easily, the Ethiopian peasants see little point in the laborious business of cultivating and pruning the plants. As a consequence much of the export coffee crop that arrives by the air cargo planes of the American-trained Ethiopian Airlines, or by rail or road, in Red Sea ports is either of a low grade or so withered or decomposed that it is unmarketable.

The *rases* made the peasants work because as landowners it was in their interests to do so. And they had the power. But now that peasant labor is no longer directly profitable to the *rases,* who will make the peasants work? Obviously, in time, the peasants will be made to understand the relationship between labor and profit; meanwhile they remain in a period of transition and, despite the potential wealth of the country, much of Ethiopia continues to go hungry.

As late as 1908 there were no schools in Ethiopia. True, there had always been a small, educated elite, but these were Amharas, most of them of noble blood, and therefore not expected to work. On assuming the throne, Haile Selassie foresaw that Ethiopia's prime need was education. Whatever his plans, they were delayed until his return from exile after the Italian occupation. By then he was doubly certain that Ethiopia could proceed no further until at least some of the ordinary people learned to

read and write. He began slowly, as is his custom, opening a school here and another there. He studied the credentials and aptitudes of the graduates carefully and those he chose for advancement were sent to universities in America and Europe, and when their studies were completed they were quickly absorbed into the government and put to work.

Education in Ethiopia remains woefully inadequate. There are too few schools and too few teachers, and those that teach are in too many cases only half-educated themselves. Of the 4 to 5 million children of school age, only some 300,000 were in school over the past few years. This figure comes from the U.S. Peace Corps and is probably closer to the truth than the more optimistic statistics provided by the Ethiopian government.

To see a rural school in operation in Ethiopia is a heartrending experience. This is not because of what goes on in the classroom (although learning by rote from a teacher who himself has learned by rote is not the most stimulating and rewarding form of instruction), but because of what goes on outside. The school may contain perhaps two hundred students. But while these are inside, memorizing their lessons, hundreds more wait outside, squatting patiently on their haunches, listening to the faint drone of voices from inside. They have been told that it is useless for them to wait, that it would be better for them to go home, or go to work. But they come anyway, day after day, because they know that without an education their future is without hope.

For the lucky few who secure a foothold on the first rung of the educational ladder, the climb to the top is a perilous one. Not many make it. As in most of Africa, an almost savage weeding-out process starts in the lower grades and continues through secondary school. With each passing year fewer survive. Of the total number of Ethiopian children receiving some form of education, less than 5 percent are enrolled in secondary schools or institutions of higher learning.

If the weeding-out process were designed solely to eliminate the dullards, it might seem less harsh. Yet more often than not the survivors are not the brighter youngsters, but children whose parents have influence and means. And in Ethiopia influence, in the final analysis, is measured in terms of the emperor.

Since the Second World War, Ethiopia has accumulated a substantial body of young men and women with university degrees. They are the new elite, the apple of the emperor's eye. In a very real sense they are his creation and dependent on him for jobs and favors. Yet in creating this growing class of educated young people, the emperor has also created a monster. It is not a monolithic monster. The emperor has seen to that. Many of the favored are deeply grateful to him for positions they now hold. There are others, however, who have been slighted or who, after a period of study in Europe or America, have returned to Ethiopia with new sets of values and new ways of looking at old problems. These are the restive ones, impatient with the parsimonious distribution of progress and reform.

True, the emperor has given Ethiopia its first constitution and its first parliament. But it was Haile Selassie who "gave" them to Ethiopia much in the way he "gave" Ethiopia its first university (Haile Selassie I University). To the young graduates, it is all too apparent that what the emperor gives he can also take away. They illustrate this by pointing out that in the early 1960's the emperor's cabinet decreed that restive students would no longer be permitted direct access to the library shelves in the university college and that all students' hostels in the capital would be closed. Student dissent has since grown belligerent, and official crackdowns correspondingly harsh. Free discussion in Ethiopia is exercised at the emperor's discretion and it is none too free. In the sixties, too, it was decreed that the punishment for "insults, abuses, defamations or slanders of the Emperor" be thirty lashes. There is no press freedom to speak of and newspapers must carry the emperor's name first in stories even if his connection to the events described is remote. References to the emperor in the third person singular are capitalized.

Strangely enough, much of the free discussion which does take place *sotto voce* in private homes or public places is mild. It is agreed that the emperor will have to go; he will not be overthrown in a spirit of vengeance, however, but with regret, as when a much-prized race horse which has broken its leg is destroyed by its trainer. On the other hand, the emperor, born in 1891, cannot live forever.

The students seated around the restaurant table with the visitor talk mostly milk-and-water conspiracy. They possess none of the single-minded toughness of true conspirators. There is too much disagreement among them, too little sense of a common purpose. Already, it seems, the farseeing emperor has riddled their ranks with potential defectors. Because he has done it with such consummate skill and so often in the past, one knows that he will smell out the potential ring leaders and, after their graduation, send them not to jail but to Ethiopia's embassies in Europe, where they will be out of touch, grow fat and become dependent on the emperor for continued advancement.

The students talk. Ten years, even five years ago the emperor led the nation. He was ahead of everyone in his thinking. Now the new elite is ahead of him. He is an old man. He does not understand the new ways. There must be a great upheaval in Ethiopia, a true and fundamental revolution. The emperor will not permit the formation of political parties; his free elections are a travesty; his parliament consists of toadies who do his bidding. . . .

It is all true and yet, as they talk, the students reveal a fatal flaw. What they really want is something not for Ethiopia as a whole but for themselves—for the new elite. Ask them whether they plan to take their education and their new-found skills into the distant provinces and there, with their sleeves rolled up, work among the peasants,

Opposite: Amhara farmer winnows
teff, Ethiopia's staple grain,
with shovel of ancient design.
Landscape (above) is typical:
houses are wattle and thatch,
fields verdant but overgrazed.
Somali girl hand-waters cattle;
animals otherwise drink at mud
holes and often become mired.

and they change the subject. No, what they seek is a rearrangement of the power structure in Addis Ababa, a juggling of plum jobs. And it is here that the emperor has them beaten, for if anyone knows the labyrinthine corridors that must be penetrated to achieve a successful palace revolution, he does.

They have tried now and then—dissident elements of the army and government and Eritrean rebels—to overthrow Selassie. In December, 1960, while he was away in Brazil, they attempted a *coup d'état*. But it fell apart because the participants disagreed among themselves, because the emperor knew too much, and because it never became (it never had a chance of becoming) a popular revolution. The peasant, the man in the street did not care. All this plotting and shooting in the streets was taking place among soldiers and officers and men who lived in houses surrounded by high walls. It did not involve him. Other, lesser bids up to the present time have been equally abortive.

The lights from the outside world pierce the shadows of Ethiopia, heralding change. Yet it is the kind of light that passes through a stained-glass window, gentle and diffused. There are just such windows in the headquarters of the Organization for African Unity in Addis Ababa. Haile Selassie commissioned them as, indeed, he commissioned the building, thus bringing all of Africa with all her disruptive passions and all her tumultuous hungers and needs into the heart of his empire. Men sit in the light cast by the giant stained-glass windows and listen while the emperor, his very presence enveloping the O.A.U. chamber in a cathedral hush, tells them about patience and moderation and the dangers of changes made too swiftly and without the necessary preparation.

In Africa now, the emperor's words are not always popular gospel. They do not lend themselves to militant banners, nor can they be carried home as palliatives for a restive people. Why then do other Africans listen? They listen because, looking about them, they notice that many of their number who preached impatience and immoderation are no longer present: Kwame Nkrumah, Patrice Lumumba, Ahmed Ben Bella. Each year the list grows longer. And they listen because they respect the emperor if for no other reason than his ability to survive. He has survived an invasion by a modern army; he has survived a European occupation, and he has survived an attempted *coup d'état* planned by his own people. In short, he has survived as emperor longer than many African leaders have been alive and that, in the African context, is a major achievement. Backed now by a 45,000-strong American-trained and equipped army, he is likely to survive even longer.

If Ethiopia is Africa's remote monastery, Liberia is its brazen honky-tonk. A ragtime melody drowns out the gentle church bells, and the aroma of incense is obliterated by cigar smoke. The courtly bow is replaced by a special handshake—opposing palms slapped together, a firm grip followed by a snapping of thumbs and fingers. "Gimme some skin, man." They talk this way here, an out-of-date American Negro slang, reminiscent of the thirties.

Like Greeks, they all seem to have cousins in Chicago and Baltimore. Do not look for African roots here, for these are Americans, the descendants of American Negro slaves. As such they are twice removed from Africa. They call themselves Americo-Liberians or Libero-Americans and it is only recently that they have begun to think of themselves as an integral and meaningful part of the rest of Africa. They still refer to the original inhabitants of their country—tribesmen like the Mandingo, the Kru, the Vai, the Buzi, and the Gola—as "aborigines," although now they are told that the official policy is one of "agglutination."

Liberia's currency is the U.S. dollar; its flag is a replica of the Stars and Stripes except that it carries only one star and eleven stripes, and its motto (inscribed on the state seal) is: "The Love of Liberty Brought Us Here."

Liberia was founded in 1822 by freed slaves sponsored by the American Colonization Society, a curious blend of northern abolitionists and southern slave owners. Their motives were mixed. The plight of the freed slaves troubled the consciences of the Northerners, and the Southerners feared "seditious" elements among them would spread the spirit of revolt among the slaves. Nonetheless, they shared a common goal: to find a home for freed American Negroes in Africa or South America. The first attempt to establish a colony, in 1820, ended in failure when three white agents and a party of eighty-eight freemen landed on Sherbro Island, off the coast of Sierra Leone. Within a matter of weeks the white men were dead of fever, as were twenty-nine of the Negroes. A year later another agent of the American Colonization Society, Dr. Eli Ayres, brought the sloop *Alligator* to Providence Island, off Cape Mesurado, the site of the present-day capital of Monrovia (named after President James Monroe). For a few hundred dollars' worth of cloth, tobacco, beads, bullets, powder, kegs of rum, and armloads of umbrellas, he purchased a 130-mile stretch of coast of unspecified depth from the local chiefs and settled the survivors of the previous expedition and one hundred and fourteen others brought directly from the United States on the steamy, fever-ridden shoreline. A similar repatriation took place in 1822, south of Monrovia, its citizens calling their inhospitable piece of geography Maryland-in-Liberia and their capital Harper. As in Monrovia to the north, their first governors were white Americans.

The early years were grim ones. The local chiefs, insisting that they had sold only the use of their land and not the land itself to the settlers, attempted to drive them out, but the new arrivals fought them off with cannon fire.

As wards of private philanthropic corporations, the new settlements found their very existence challenged by the governments

of England and France. The United States, not wishing to become embroiled in geographical disputes in far-off Africa, refused to declare a protectorate. To help clear the situation, the American Colonization Society stepped out of the picture in 1847 and the Monrovia settlement (followed ten years later by Maryland-in-Liberia) became the Republic of Liberia.

If the first years were grim ones, they were also brave and ennobling as the intrepid settlers battled hunger, disease, and hostile natives for their survival. But the decades that followed were neither brave nor ennobling.

Now that their fathers had cleared the land, the children set about making themselves comfortable. They built large plantation homes, reminiscent of the antebellum South, dressed themselves in top hats and striped trousers, and danced the quadrille and the Virginia Reel. Disdaining manual labor, they took up the practice of law and politics and hailed each other into the courts for the sheer joy of litigation. They spent money like fools and their governments floated loans with private European and American investors at incredible rates of interest. Often the nation's creditors came close to foreclosing and, during the course of the years, Liberia lost large chunks of its territory (estimates vary from 10 to 60 percent) to the neighboring colonies of Sierra Leone, Guinea, and the Ivory Coast.

Most disgraceful of all was the attitude of the settlers toward the original inhabitants. It seemed as if the Libero-Americans had remembered nothing of their own recent encounter with slavery or had learned all the wrong lessons. For when it came to the one million or so unagglutinated aborigines of the interior, the Americo-Liberians either ignored them or enslaved them.

A League of Nations report,* published a little over eighty years after the birth of the Republic, makes horrifying reading. The report found that slavery, as defined by the antislavery convention, continued to exist in Liberia and that contract laborers "were recruited under conditions of criminal compulsion scarcely distinguishable from slave trading." The report deeply implicated high officials of the government in the forcible exportation of Liberian tribesmen to the French Gabon and the Spanish island of Fernando Po, a thousand miles to the south.

Aside from the exportation of forced labor, the League commission unearthed other practices: "pawning" and forced labor within Liberia itself. Pawning meant pawning human beings—oneself, one's own child, or a relative—in payment for a bad debt. The League commission was told of persons who had spent years of their lives in pawn and of women who were taken as pawns "to attract male labor" on plantations.

In the aftermath of these and other disclosures, the president and vice-president of Liberia were forced to resign, but not before (or so it is strongly rumored) hundreds of tribesmen who had testified before the League commission

---

* Report of the International Commission of Inquiry into the Existence of Slavery and Forced Labor in the Republic of Liberia (Washington, U.S. Government Printing Office, 1931).

What Ethiopia is, rate at which it progresses, and direction it goes are determined by absolute monarch, Emperor Haile Selassie (below). Stylized Lion of Judah in Addis Ababa is national symbol. Coptic church is in south, on way to Harrar. Painting of Abyssinian cavalry is at Gondar.

had been liquidated.

For the oldest independent black republic in Africa, the decade of the twenties was surely its historical nadir. The British, righteously revolted by reports of slavery and forced labor, were calling for the dismemberment of the republic and its replacement with "strong, high-minded white men." Financially, Liberia's condition was parlous. At one point in the twenties its debts absorbed 67 percent of the national revenue and the government owed $1.7 million to French, British, German, and United States bankers. Seemingly unable to make even a tentative stab at putting its house in order, Liberia continued to lead the life of a profligate escapist. In 1929 its government spent more on brass bands than it did on public health, and one president of Monrovia's only institution of higher learning (it claimed to be a university although for years it had no library, laboratories, or scientific equipment) sent his daughters to schools in Italy, financing this excursion with the entire budget of the "university's" education department.

By rights the Americo-Liberians should have perished like the grasshoppers in the fable. But providence in the form of a "strong, high-minded white man" named Harvey S. Firestone saved them in the nick of time. Firestone's mind was on rubber (a place to grow enough of it and cheaply enough to break the monopoly of British planters in Malaya and Sumatra) and, in return for a Firestone agreement to buy enough Liberian gold bonds to set-

tle the government's outstanding debts, the Liberian government agreed to lease to Firestone up to one million acres of land for ninety-nine years.

In his memorandum of agreement with President King (written before the explosive League of Nations report was made public), Firestone blazed an unprecedented trail in Liberian labor relations. "Labor," he wrote the undoubtedly mystified Liberian president, "shall be free to bargain for its terms and shall be free to sever its employment with the Company at its own will and convenience."

The arrival of Firestone in 1926 marked the turning point in the fortunes of Liberia. Two years before the Firestone program got under way, Liberia was totally undeveloped. There was not a single payroll in the entire country. By the 1960's Firestone alone employed some 26,000 workers, had 90,000 acres planted in rubber trees, and remained Liberia's principal golden-egg-laying goose.

Government policy is to coddle the goose, encourage it to lay as many eggs as possible, and entice other geese to do the same. Sometimes this policy conflicts with the aspirations of Liberians who work for these companies, and when it does the geese and the eggs come first and those who tend them second. As an example, in February of 1966, approximately 10,000 Firestone latex gatherers went on strike for higher wages. They did so despite a warning from Liberia's president that such a walkout would be illegal. The president, worried by the *coups d'état* in black Africa, and even more worried by the possibility that the Firestone goose might pick up its eggs and go elsewhere, instructed his legislature to pass a law authorizing him to forbid strikes that threatened state security. The law also prohibited Liberian labor unions (still weak and ineffectively led) from receiving financial aid from abroad without the government's permission, and empowered the president to suspend habeas corpus proceedings in dealing with "illegal" walkouts.

Similarly, the government has placed its protective arm over other foreign corporate investors. At last count there were thirty-eight major foreign companies working in Liberia with a total investment of approximately $750 million. These concessionaires are the country's major employers and the revenue produced by them accounts for half of the gross domestic product. At the same time, the Liberians are producing more under their own steam. Firestone is still the leading producer of rubber, but independent Liberian output has increased to nearly half of Firestone's total, a rise of 300 percent in less than a decade.

In varying degrees, most of the foreign companies in Liberia have followed the guidelines laid down by the Firestone company and practice a benevolent, almost colonial brand of paternalism. Firestone itself has built and equipped two hospitals and thirty-nine dispensaries staffed by twelve physicians and surgeons. Its annual medical budget runs close to $1 million. Firestone has also built schools, conducts an adult education program, encourages individual Liberian entrepreneurs to grow rubber, and supports charitable institutions.

Firestone (and the other foreign companies) also supports William Vacanarat Shadrach Tubman, the eighteenth president of Liberia and leader of the nation's only political party, the True Whigs. To do otherwise in Liberia would be to practice a nihilistic philosophy incompatible with free enterprise. *Laissez-faire* capitalism thrives in Liberia at President Tubman's pleasure.

As Haile Selassie is Ethiopia, so septuagenarian Tubman is Liberia. Having served several consecutive terms as president, Tubman governs Liberia much in the manner of an old-time big-city politician in "the States," through personality, perseverance, and patronage.

The government of Liberia is modeled along American lines. The legislative bodies are called the House of Representatives and the Senate, and there is a Supreme Court which, in theory, is independent of the legislative and executive branches. Liberians are permitted to vote, and do, but only for the president, vice-president, and members of the House and the Senate. District commissioners, diplomats, police chiefs, army officers and other senior officials owe their jobs to the president. Job-holders who do not please the president do not hold jobs for long.

Tubman does not "win" his elections. Rather, he re-enacts them in the style

Liberia: Hardship and corruption marked first century of existence for oldest independent republic in Africa, but exports of rubbe and iron ore (right and bottom) help stabilize economy today. Monrovia the capital, has cylindrical—and handsome—Ministry of Justice, as well as traditional street bazaar.

of an Oberammergau Passion Play, the quadriennial rites calling for complete and wholehearted co-operation of the citizenry. Real opposition is unthinkable and its practitioners are banished or broken. At times, however, curiosity impels the president to see what it is like to campaign against an opponent, and he has arranged to have one run against him. In one such election he was opposed by a former judge and part-time church organist who said, in the course of his campaign, that he was "not particularly opposed" to President Tubman, but was campaigning "in response to the ardent desire of Dr. Tubman for fair and friendly competition." On election day, Tubman received 530,566 votes and his co-operative antagonist 41.

Diagrammed on paper, the government of Liberia resembles not so much a table of organization as it does a family tree. With few exceptions, office holders (judges, court clerks, cabinet ministers, and the like) are related to one another. It is nepotism on a grand scale, although perhaps it is an excusable nepotism because, until recently, the only Liberians who could read and write and thus qualify for jobs in the administration were Americo-Liberians. Being a small group (variously estimated at between twenty and thirty thousand), they could not help being related to one another. The exceptions—their un-westernized names stand out among the Yancys, Tubmans, Barclays, Talberts, Shermans, and Brewers—are the tribal Africans. The man responsible for their presence in the government structure is President Tubman. Until Tubman took office in 1944 no Liberian president had cared or dared to penetrate into the interior. Emissaries of the administration who did travel more than forty miles from the coastline were usually involved in the collecting of forced labor or on bloody missions of "pacification." With good reason the tribes of the hinterlands viewed the Americo-Liberians with the gravest suspicion. But President Tubman changed all that. Perhaps he agreed with his Americo-Liberian friends and advisers that the aborigines were inferior, but he did not think this was necessarily their fault and to his critics he quoted the Liberian constitution, which says in part that the purpose of Liberia is "to provide a home for the dispersed and oppressed Children of Africa, and to regenerate and enlighten this benighted Continent." There were also practical political reasons for adjusting the traditional policy toward the natives of the interior. Change was sweeping through Africa. Sooner or later it would reach the deprived and despised majority of his own constituency. Unless he managed—and quickly—to become their leader, they would chose one of their own and through sheer weight of numbers force him out. So the new president, doffing top hat and cutaway and donning native garb, began to tour the unfamiliar corners of his country, establishing schools and clinics, replacing oppressive and unpopular government officials with more responsive ones, and preaching the gospel of "agglutination." Agglutination, of course, meant joining the True Whig party, but what Tubman offered was more than had ever been offered before and the tribesmen seized it hungrily.

The health of a political machine is directly related to the number of jobs and favors it dispenses. To grow, the machine must dispense even more jobs and favors. A few years ago, in explaining to an interviewer the philosophy of his open-door policy, President Tubman said: "We will not go hat in hand to beg. We are not for sale."

But if Liberia is not for sale (only blacks can become citizens and only citizens can own land), it is most certainly for rent —its land, its resources, its people. Even its flag is for rent. Through low registration fees and comparatively unregulated working conditions, Liberia has accumulated one of the world's largest commercial fleets. The ships are mostly Greek- or American-owned (none is owned by Liberian nationals), but they fly the Star and Strips of Liberia and contribute heavily to the national treasury.

The Tubman open-door policy has transformed Liberia. In the decade of the fifties the government's income increased more than 500 percent. Since 1951 the wage labor force has jumped threefold, the number of classroom seats fourfold, and the miles of all-weather roads sixfold. And all this where less than a generation ago three-quarters of the population could not speak the national language (let alone read or write it) and, since there were quite literally no roads, travelers had to tramp on foot or be carried by "pawns" in hammocks. It is astonishing and gratifying, and yet, almost in geometrical proportion to the improvements, the pressures increase. There are pressures from the Americo-Liberians to place more of their number in the top management positions currently held by white men, although the whites say too few of them are qualified. There are pressures from the aborigines to break down the social, economic, and political walls erected by the Americo-Liberians, and a consequent defensive rush to the barricades on the part of the Americo-Liberians. Greatest of all is the pressure among the growing body of workers for a greater share of the profits divided between the foreign investors and the True Whig government.

Underlying everything is the reality of corruption. To accomplish anything, somebody must be bribed. Leech-like, government officials attach themselves to the boards of the foreign companies. Corruption is so prevalent and is engaged in so openly and by so many that it has become almost respectable.

One is tempted to shrug it off. Liberia is not alone. There is corruption everywhere in the world. But it is not just corruption. It is all the other things too—the autocrat supported by foreign capitalists; corruption at the highest levels; suppression of the opposition; a rich aristocracy and a restive proletariat and peasantry. And suddenly there seems to be a parallel. Is this Cuba before Castro?

189

WORLD OF THE BROWN PEOPLE

the sands of the Sahara isolate the coastal region of the Mediterranean Sea from the immense land mass of Africa below the equator. Whether called the Western Desert of Egypt, or the Libyan Desert in Libya, this sandy ocean is all, in effect, the Sahara, stretching from the Red Sea to the Atlantic. It is broken only once in the whole of its 3,600-mile span: where the Nile spills over from the lakes of the Central African highlands, tumbles into the plain, and cuts a narrow swath of reverberating greenness northward through wilderness to reach the Mediterranean, some 4,200 miles away. It is a measure of the barrenness of its course that not a single tributary joins the river in the final 1,700 miles of its journey through the Sudan and Egypt to the sea. Only on the Nile is there any partial merging of peoples; elsewhere all contact is attenuated by the desert, where small and scattered populations cultivate tiny oases or wander endlessly as nomads in a pitiless environment. It is common practice to recognize this great division in the continent by speaking of people "north of the Sahara" or "south of the Sahara," and, broadly speaking, it is the former who are the Arabs.

There was a time when the Sahara was a vast, verdant prairie nourished by rivers and numerous people lived there. It was the withdrawal of the ice cap northward from Europe about fifteen thousand years ago that wrought the change, for the rain-bearing winds of the Atlantic which had fallen on North Africa were drawn into Europe as its frozen body was warmed back to life. The prairies of North Africa withered in the waterless heat and the people slowly dispersed in search of life-giving water. Some went south and were merged and lost in the Negrito races there; some crossed the sea into the islands of the Mediterranean and to Europe; some journeyed east into the valley of the Nile.

All except those who went south were later to be identified by anthropologists as "the Mediterranean type," or "brown people," which is the basic racial stock of North Africa. There is evidence of the distance they traveled in their early migrations in the fact that Bretons, Irish, Welsh, Cornish, and other people on the Atlantic coast of northwest Europe still show racial affinities with them. Those who remained in North Africa were contained and protected by desert and sea. Many thousands of years ago the first primitive societies formed in East Africa tried to descend by the Nile, but prehistoric remains found in Nubia suggest that they halted in the harsh, inhospitable cataract region, which stretches 450 miles southward from Aswan. Here the valley consists of harsh cliffs broken by plains of sand that roll down to the water's edge and the river flows over a broken and rocky bed. It was a natural and visible frontier which closed the one gateway to North Africa for a long and uncharted period of time.

The Arabs of contemporary North Africa are, therefore, the people on the northern Nile and the North African coast, most of the nomads of the desert, and the settled farmers of the oases. Over thousands of years the basic Mediterranean type has been modified by the influx of settlers and conquerors, but its members are still bound together by the religion and social customs of Islam and by the Arabic language. The Arabs do not acknowledge minor racial differences, such as those of the Berbers of northwest Africa. To them all people whose language is Arabic are Arabs. This language and identity were brought to them in the seventh century—late in the history of a region which had seen Egypt in its glory four thousand years before and had lived under Phoenicia and the Greco-Romans for two millennia—by nomads from the Arabian desert. By comparison with the city dwellers of North Africa, the invaders were socially primitive people newly emerged from paganism, but they toppled older and more sophisticated civilizations in Europe and Asia until the Arab empire controlled far more of the world than did Rome at its zenith.

The submission of an advanced society to a less-developed people is not without precedent, but it is remarkable that North Africa committed itself permanently to the Arabs. The reason it did lies in the spiritual fervor in which it was gripped from the beginning. The Arabs, although newly turned from paganism, brought with them a rich language and a simple faith; they burst from the mindless desert in which they had sheltered their poverty for thousands of years into a world already advanced in arts and crafts, in intellect, in systems of government and trade which they had to learn almost from the beginning. They only had the civilizing influence of the Prophet Mohammed's vision of the one God to lift them from their recent past toward the conglomerate wisdom of the world they entered. Undoubtedly it was the vigor of the new and active faith which determined the outcome, for throughout the world there are now nearly 400 million practicing Moslems. But whereas peoples to the east of Arabia retained their languages and racial name and traits, North Africa was different. In North Africa, regardless of background, the people call themselves Arabs, use the Arabic language, and profess Islam.

Historically, Islam is the third monotheistic religion after Judaism and Christianity, and is in fact derived from them. Jesus Christ is the second prophet of Islam after Mohammed, and a Moslem could accept a great part of Christian doctrine without apostasizing. It was strange that the Egyptians and the other North Africans, who were for the most part Christian at the time of the Arab conquest, should have been so willing to abandon one monotheistic faith for another; yet they did. There are many differences in physical characteristics, social customs, and politics to be found in a journey from Cairo to Casablanca, but Islam makes all peoples it touches one.

In the beginning, North Africans accepted Islam largely in opposition to earlier conquerors who had brought and imposed Christianity on them. The Coptic, Monophysitic church of Egypt became the focal point of national resistance both to the Christian church of Byzantium and to By-

zantine rule. The Coptic church has survived into the present day in Egypt and Ethiopia, but the Copts are now a minority religious group and the Coptic language (a survival of ancient Egyptian) exists only in the sanctuaries of the church and the monasteries.

The Copts are supposed to be the true descendants of the ancient Egyptians, but a great many Egyptian Moslems are also descended from the indigenous inhabitants of the Nile Valley, for over the centuries the great majority turned to Islam and became the clients of their Arab conquerors. Even more important in changing racial characteristics, the Arabs themselves "assimilated to their creed, speech and even physical type, more aliens than any stock before or since, not excepting the Hellenic, the Roman, the Anglo-Saxon or the Russian." * It is for this reason that the Arabs themselves tend to define Arabs as people who speak Arabic. Generally, the only "true Arabs" are said to be found in the deserts of Arabia; all others have intermarried with other racial groups or descended from other racial stock. It may well be, however, that many tribes in the North African deserts are of the same racial type because thousands of years ago the people in the Arabian peninsula, except for those on the southern and eastern coasts, were also of the Mediterranean type. Certainly the desert people of Cyrenaica consider themselves to be truly Arab.

This cannot be true of most of the townspeople in Egypt or the cities and towns along the North African coast. Indeed, in Egypt most Copts and many Moslems reject a racial identity with the Arabs. One could also throw some doubt on their claim to be pure Egyptians, because long before Alexander the Great conquered Egypt in 332 B.C. there had been a great influx of Greek traders and foreign mercenaries who settled in the country and became Egyptian nationals. All along the coast west of the Nile delta, the towns and cities had either been conquered by foreigners or created by foreigners, as the great ruins, such as the Greek city of Cyrene or the vast Roman city of Leptis Magna, bear witness.

The Phoenicians from the coast of Lebanon and Palestine settled towns in Tripolitania, Tunisia, and Algeria which endured for many centuries before the Arabs arrived. Leptis Magna once provided an emperor for Rome: Septimus Severus, a great warrior who died in England and is buried at York. Carthage, in Tunisia, eventually became independent of the Phoenician homeland, and its soldiers and ships pushed around the northern coast of Africa to establish their power as far west as Morocco. Long after the Arab conquest, the people from Tripoli westward to the Atlantic coast were Berbers and their terrain became famous as the Barbary Coast, home of the great pirate nation. Their origins are not known but they were almost certainly descendants of the light-skinned Mediterranean type. The ancient Berber language is still spoken in the mountain areas of Morocco and clearly has affinities with the language once used in Libya, for it has helped to decipher antique Libyan wall inscriptions. If there

* D. G. Hogarth, *The Penetration of Arabia,* New York, 1904.

Salt-laden camels walk at rate
of 3km per hour, may cover up
to 50kms a day. Barren Hoggar
mountains of southern Algeria
are citadel for Tuareg caravan
marauders. Opposite: Village of
Iferouane, in Aïr mountains of
Niger, enjoys milder existence
farming fertile savannah land.

is added to the conquests and settlements of Phoenicians, Romans and Greeks, the subsequent conquests and settlements by Arabs, Turks, and eventually Europeans, it becomes evident that the people of North Africa today cannot have much Arab stock in them. But their language and Islam, having survived through nearly twelve centuries, have imposed on them the characteristics of Arabs, and given them their place in the community of Arabs.

Contemporary North Africans all call themselves Arab, but the Egyptian is still very conscious of being Egyptian and a Berber will still tell you proudly that he is a Berber. And just as the Nile Valley imposed distinctive characteristics on its people, so the Atlas mountains of Morocco, whose three great ranges trap the rain-bearing winds and provide rivers and fertility in the valleys and on the mountain slopes, divide the inhabitants from the desert people behind and do much to sustain Berber customs and traditions. The Moroccans have also been greatly affected by their association with Spain during and after the Arab empire. They were largely responsible for the conquest of Spain but, in turn, the music, architecture, and customs of Andalusia came back to Morocco. To this day the folk music of Andalusia is part of the Moroccan heritage.

The final impact made by conquest came from Europe. The French began their occupation of Algeria early in the nineteenth century and progressively tightened their hold on the three Maghreb countries (Morocco, Algeria, Tunisia), which they did much to modernize. The great cities of Casablanca, Rabat, Marrakesh, Fez, Algiers, and Tunis were enlarged and Europeanized, and the extensive network of broad and good roads was constructed. Of even greater importance, the French imposed their culture and language. Tunis, Algiers, Rabat, and Casablanca are very much "French" towns, and the French language is for many people their first language. French newspapers are more widely read than the Arabic press, most of which has existed only since the three countries got their independence.

Despite the fact that Britain was the dominant power associated with Egypt from 1882 until 1956, Egypt retains a number of French characteristics and there are many among the older, impoverished "aristocrats" of Egyptian society whose second language is French. Mohammed Aly the Great, the Albanian-born commander of Albanian troops in Ottoman Egypt, who became pasha in 1805 after helping the nationalists rid the country of the hated Turks, was francophile and established in both the economic and military fields the influence of France. As he ruled Egypt for forty-two years, the influence persisted long after the British had become the dominant power. French was the polite language of the court and the pashas, and the architecture in the cities and towns of Egypt was largely French in style. Only in the last quarter century has English taken command because the geographical extent of the English-speaking peoples and the leading role of the United States clearly made it necessary for Egyptians to become familiar with the language.

The western half of Libya —Tripolitania—has many characteristics of Italy, partly because of the proximity of the two countries but mainly because Tripolitania was occupied by the Italians in the early part of this century. As with the French in Maghreb, so in Libya the Italians embarked on vast programs of settlement, and ancient Tripoli became the capital of an Italian province. Modern Tripoli is very much an Italian city, with broad streets and arcaded shopping quarters, but the old towns stand out boldly on the western end of the harbor, dominated by a fine old fort which is now a museum.

These historical connections have dictated to a large extent both the characteristics and the politics of the region. With the exception of Lebanon, the educated North African Arabs identify more closely with Europe than do the Middle Eastern Arabs; they breathe from the Mediterranean and not from the eastern deserts. Morocco, Algeria, and Tunisia bear the unmistakable stamp of French culture, Tripolitania of Italy, Cyrenaica and Egypt of Britain. Their political radicalism derives in the main from European concepts of individual freedom and social justice, and if some of the Arab leaders now lean heavily on Soviet Russia it is not because they are Marxist ideologues but because Russia has always been willing to exert its own influence against that of the Western powers, and to this end has helped them conduct their wars of liberation and arm themselves for the continuing struggle with Israel.

The European influence in Africa is considerably diluted today. Morocco's long history of monarchy has given its people—despite the domestic opposition that from time to time exerts itself—a stable type of monarchical rule. To that extent it is now the most conservative regime in North Africa. Egypt, on the other hand, thought of its monarchy and its aristocracy as foreign; and in truth, until Farouk, its kings spoke French or Turkish much more than they spoke Arabic. The national movement was Egyptian and it only took the combination of King Farouk's degeneracy and the revolt of the army to bring the dynasty and the power of the aristocracy to an end in 1952. The eighteen-year rule of King Idriss of Libya never properly took root in the country, and its intense conservatism and the corruption that surrounded the palace at a time of increasing radical nationalism inevitably led to the army revolt in 1969 which put Libya in the ranks of the "progressive" Arab regimes under Egypt's leadership. The situation in the Sudan has been different only in background. The British implanted parliamentary government after its own fashion in a country without tradition or experience to run it, and it was the continuing ineffectiveness of this government that led, again, to an army revolt and a left-wing military oligarchy.

The Moroccan monarchy at the present time can count with confidence only on Tunisia for political support, and then only because the moderation and wisdom of the Tunisian nationalist leader and president, Habib Bourguiba, has re-

Troupe of skilled belly dancers performs on colorful mosaic of Moroccan carpets at coronation feast in High Atlas mountains. Girls are from Khénifra, town noted for excellently trained dancers. Opposite: Overview of sparkling white Tunisian town with dominant square minaret.

sisted the extreme, radical blandishments of Egypt, Algeria, and Russia. Egypt, Sudan, Libya, and Algeria are all pseudosocialist and "progressive" states fundamentally opposed to monarchy.

The currents of political thought, however, are not all in the same direction. The older and more progressive the states become, the more they tend toward a middle position. If it had not been for Egypt's total dependence on Russia for arms against Israel, President Nasser very likely would have slanted his policy more toward the West in the two or three years before his death, and most Egyptians would welcome such a policy if it were possible. Algeria, which is about two thousand miles from Israel, has weakened its Soviet connection in recent years and has still the powerful and now traditional connection with France, which Morocco and Tunisia retain. The young officers of the Sudan and Libya are still in the first fine flush of their power and radicalism, but their power is of doubtful durability and their people ill-suited to a communistic society.

Arab Africa presents a picture of the new world superimposed on layers of history. This is true even in the characteristics of the people, for the Europeanized people of the main cities from Cairo to Casablanca are sophisticated, dress in European clothes, have acquired European customs and habits, and are often as lax in their observance of the strict rules of Islam as any Westerner might be in his practice of Christianity. Usually the old parts of the cities huddle in the middle or perch on the outskirts of the contemporary complex. In Cairo the old town strings out toward the south, with some of its ancient walls and the 1,300-year-old Al Aqsa Mosque still to be seen. Egyptian handicrafts, silverwork, jewelry, and the scents and herbs of the country are sold from small shops and stalls in a labyrinth of narrow streets which seems to culminate in another venerable building, the Blue Mosque. These *souks*, or markets, are commonly found somewhere in all the old cities—in Algiers, in Marrakesh, around the harbor and the fort at Rabat, in Fez, and in the Turkish town of Tripoli. They are the haunts of tourists who, though they stay in the fine new hotels in the new cities, find the exotic they are seeking in the old.

The dominance of Islam is kept perpetually in mind by the mosques, which are seldom out of sight. Many of them are works of great beauty. The very old ones are usually simple and austere in design; others are more ornate but still graceful. Their design usually reflects a period of history, as in the case of the great time of building during the Mameluke rule in Egypt, or when the Moors were dominant in the Maghreb.

The farther one departs from the modern cities, whether it is deep into the old *souks* or into the countryside, the more one goes back in time to the "arabism" of the region. This is partially disguised in Libya and in the Maghreb, where fruit and olive groves in their orderly, parallel lines of trees stretching into the distance bear witness to the period of Italian and French settlement. Even the farmhouses have the appearance of those to be found in Italy and France. But since the vast majority of settlers have now departed from North Africa, the Europeanization is deceptive. The Arabs are preserving their own customs, traditions, and family habits in houses where foreigners once lived.

European dress becomes more and more rare as the traveler journeys from the city. Although there are many costumes, they are mostly variations of the *kaftan* (cloak), the *galabieh* (the long white shirt), the *keffiyeh* (the headshawl), and the *agal* (the cord holding the headshawl in position). These were and are typically the dress of the desert Arabs. The red fez, introduced from Turkey during the Ottoman empire, has virtually disappeared from Egypt and is rarely to be found in the Maghreb. The Moroccans, in particular, have developed a particular costume of their own, still basically the long cloak but with a folded hat in place of the *keffiyeh*.

The Egyptians of the Nile Valley are a distinctive group. Because land is so valuable that they cannot spare a square inch more than necessary, they live crowded together in villages and this gives the impression of extreme dirtiness that travelers frequently remark upon. They are bound to their land with an extraordinary affection, so much so that a family will be reluctant to move five miles from its traditional home. Education is now breaking this down as more and more young people go away to school and see the attraction of bigger towns; they are attracted, too, by the higher wages of developing industry. There were no less than 33,000 laborers, gathered from the length and breadth of Egypt, working on the Aswan dam during the peak of construction.

The Nubians of upper Egypt and the northern Sudan are of uncertain origins, but are racially distinct from the Egyptians proper and preserve a spoken language of their own. They lived in the Nile cataract region of the two countries for more than two thousand years, settling in the occasional bays in the rocky riversides. The living offered by this harsh environment was precarious. There was little land to cultivate and the Nubians were and remain, despite their innate intelligence, very poor fishermen. Most of the young men preferred work as servants or *bawabs* (doormen) in the cities of the Sudan and Egypt. They married girls from their villages and then went back to their work, sometimes not seeing their wives for two or three years at a time. The building of the High Dam, however, submerged almost the whole of Nubia. The Egyptian Nubians were then housed in a new town at Kom Ombo, on the Nile in Upper Egypt, and the Sudanese Nubians were transported eastward to the river Atbara and resettled in new towns there.

The Sudan itself is a member of the Arab League and technically a part of Arab North Africa, but the people are racially non-Arab and only the northern half of the country uses Arabic as a first language. To the south lie tribal peoples related to those of Ethiopia, Uganda, and the Congo. Whereas the north is Moslem, the south is largely

pagan or Christian. The name Sudan means "the country of the blacks," and the "Arabs" of the north are dark-skinned people. In temperament they exhibit some of the jollity, humor, and calmness—broken by fits of laughter or occasionally of violence—that one associates with the peoples south of the Sahara.

The Berbers in the mountains and deserts of the Maghreb have also maintained a colorful separateness in their societies. Their traditions are deeply entrenched in their domestic and social customs. This is notably so of Morocco which was, by the standards of those days, an imperial power with its own dynasties for many centuries. Fez and Marrakesh in particular are the repositories of the relics of these ancient days and are filled with the ruins of palaces and mosques and mausoleums. Throughout Morocco there is great reverence for the national folklore and folk art; one of the important events of the year is the folklore festival in Marrakesh. The superb care with which Moroccan traditions are preserved reflects a respect for the past even deeper than that found in Egypt, which has a much longer recorded history. Where the high Atlas mountains maintain a degree of separation from the sophisticated life of the coastal plain, those traditions persist.

The ingrained sense of history found in Morocco is present in some degree everywhere in Arab North Africa and is essential to the comprehension of the area. Egyptians do not express it as commonly as Moroccans; they are, in general, a quiet, tolerant people, not greatly attracted to the heroics of the war now imposed on them by the conflict with Israel. Yet they are conscious of their long history and their contributions both to civilization and Islam. This gives them a firm inner conviction that as a nation they can never for long be subdued or destroyed. By contrast, the Cyrenaicans claim direct descent from the Arabs of the Arabian peninsula and this has imparted to them a more passionate and aggressive sense of their commitment both to the Arab world and to Islam.

Nevertheless, the modern world is now imposing on the region something of its more material characteristics. There is notably the growth of Arab national thought in the overall sense and secondly the recognition of each country as a "nation-state," a concept which came from Europe. Little more than a hundred years ago, Arabs everywhere thought of themselves as regional parts of the Islamic—as distinct from Arab—world, living within the Islamic Ottoman empire. Arab nationalism as such is barely sixty years old and first expressed itself simply as a desire for autonomy within the Ottoman empire. It was the break-up of the empire after 1918 and the division of the Middle East—to which North Africa was now closely related—into several countries which gave impetus to the idea of nation-states. As the strength of these individual nations grows, Arab "unity" becomes more difficult to achieve.

Nevertheless, the idea of unity is sustained by the emotional will of many

Arabs; any effort toward unification evokes an emotional response. The late President Nasser of Egypt reached the peak of his popularity when he became president of the United Arab Republic which joined Egypt and Syria together, and the collapse of this union did his reputation great harm. The 1970 "federal" union of Egypt, the Sudan, and Libya, later joined by Syria, is a concept too loose to permit definition, largely because President Nasser, before his death, decided that he would not again make the mistakes he made in 1958 in the union with Syria. He created what he considered was a concept toward growth of union, and his "collective successors" in the government of Egypt are maintaining this policy.

It remains difficult to determine which is the more artificial of the two concepts: the historical and unifying force of "arabism" or the later structure of the nationalism of nation-states. The inbred separateness of some Egyptians and Berbers has already been noted. In North Africa, the most natural division is at the Gulf of Sirte, leaving Tripolitania with the three Maghreb countries as one natural geographic and ethnic region, and to the east, Cyrenaica could more naturally be united with Egypt. This could not come about except by war, since it would mean dividing Libya, which, now rich with oil, would never agree.

The war with Israel has undoubtedly strengthened national ideology, although west of Egypt the North Africans are very conscious of it as an Islamic struggle. This is particularly true in Morocco, whose king, Hassan II, summoned the first Islamic conference in 1969 for the purpose of mobilizing the entire Moslem world against Israel. The loss of Arab Jerusalem particularly offends the Moslem character of the region.

The dominant characteristic of modern times has been the struggle for independence against the European powers, a struggle which has terminated in victory for the Arabs everywhere in North Africa except for the northern part of the Spanish Sahara colony, the small enclave of Ifni on the Atlantic coast of Morocco, and the two towns of Ceuta and Mililla, which are considered by Spain to be part of its home territory. The Spanish Sahara holds the world's most extensive lode of phosphate, with an estimated yield of 1.7 billion tons. The territory's encircling "brother" nations—Algeria, Morocco, and Mauritania—with expectations of sharing in the phosphate wealth, have long pressured Madrid to grant self-government to the 50,000 nomadic Arabs, Moors, and Berbers of her African colony, and this step is imminent.

The longest and most destructive war of independence was fought by the Algerian people. Their country had been occupied by France in the first half of the nineteenth century and later incorporated into metropolitan France. This was done at the behest of French and other foreign settlers in 1848, but it did not allay the enmity of the Algerians. The final outbreak of violence occurred in 1954 and within eighteen months young Algerians,

Sahara sandstorm: Camels have been unloaded and set free to endure in own fashion. Drivers cloak selves in blankets, will round up animals later. Berber girl in ceremonial paint wears robe in pattern of her tribe. Public scribe writes note for illiterate Marrakesh customer.

many of them trained in the French army, had recruited an army of about twenty thousand guerrillas. In time this army forced the French to use an army of 500,000 men and to fortify the long frontiers with Tunisia and Morocco. Despite this vast effort, President de Gaulle conceded independence in 1962.

Morocco was occupied by France in 1907 and immediately experienced resistance from the Moroccan people, but it was not until the memorable revolt of the Rif tribal leader, Abd el-Krim, in his home mountains in 1923 that serious difficulty was encountered, and its suppression completed the French conquest. Morocco was ruled by a long-established monarchy and after World War II the reigning sultan, Mohammed V, sided with the independence movement and was exiled by the French in 1953. This was a signal for revolt which culminated in the restoration of the monarchy in 1956. It was a bitter struggle but never achieved the violence and bloodiness of the Algerian war of independence. Independence was also achieved in Tunisia without the appalling cost of Algeria. The French established a protectorate there in 1881 with the bey, traditional ruler of the country, as a figurehead. As in other Maghreb countries, they built good new roads and harbors, but they also brought in colonists who were helped to acquire the best land and in time owned one-tenth of the entire cultivable area. The inevitable discontent led to the formation of the Young Tunisian Party in 1907, but it was not until the Neo-Destour Party was formed under the leadership of the able and intelligent Habib Bourguiba that agitation became a serious threat to the French. In subsequent years, Bourguiba spent much of his time in exile or in prison, but the French at last conceded independence in 1956. A year later the bey was deposed and Bourguiba became president.

Libya was occupied by the Italians in 1911, but for many years their rule did not extend much further than the coastal strip of Tripolitania and they were forced to recognize the rule of the powerful Senussi order in Cyrenaica. The Italians did not keep to this agreement because they sought more land for their colonists, and as a result were faced with a serious revolt in the late twenties which ended only when the Libyan national hero, Omar al-Mukhtar, was caught and executed in 1931. Many Libyans then left the country, mostly for Egypt, where Idriss, chief of the Senussi, was also in exile. These emigrants volunteered for service with the British in the desert war of 1939. The Allied victory finally drove the Italians out of the country, and the United Nations General Assembly recognized the rights of the Libyans to independence. In 1951 Idriss became the first king of what was then a federal state consisting of the two main provinces of Tripolitania and Cyrenaica, and of Fezzan, a small group of oases deep inland near the Tunisian frontier. In 1963 it became a unitary state under a central government.

Except for five years from 1917, when Britain declared a protectorate, Egypt was not in theory ruled by Britain. But in practice the Brit-

214

ish consul-general was the ruler of the country from the occupation in 1882 until the Anglo-Egyptian Treaty of Independence in 1936; and even after that the British ambassador was a dominant influence in the country until the end of World War II. The Egyptian national movement was well established from the turn of the century, but it sought its ends mainly by political means and except for a big revolt against the protectorate in 1919, consisted in the main of sporadic and brief outbreaks of violence and occasional assassinations. The British gradually relinquished the rights they had acquired for themselves in 1882, so there was no precise point at which Egypt became totally independent, but the final act came in 1954 when the British negotiated with the new revolutionary government for the withdrawal of British troops from the Suez Canal zone, which they had occupied to safeguard the canal by right of the 1936 treaty. The withdrawal was completed in 1956.

The Sudan has been another part of the Egyptian story, for it was an Egyptian possession in the nineteenth century. The Mahdi rebellion, forever associated with General Charles George ("Chinese") Gordon, who died defending Khartoum, broke this link for some years, and when General Kitchener reconquered the country in 1898 the British imposed a "condominium," which was in theory joint rule by Britain and Egypt. Britain nevertheless continued to administer the Sudan alone and not until 1953 did Britain, Egypt, and Sudanese delegates negotiate the country's independence.

The effect of these struggles for independence along the coast of North Africa was to create "national movements" which became the dominant influence in each country in turn. They all shared the general philosophy of Arab nationalism, which was pro-Islam and therefore anticommunist, but was always radical. Its aims became "freedom, unity, and socialism," but the socialism, being national in concept, was opposed to the internationalism of Marxist-Leninist doctrines. The national movement was also fundamentally opposed to kingship, which has very shallow roots in the Arab world, and it was therefore not surprising that in the 1952 revolution of Gamal Abdul Nasser in Egypt King Farouk lost his throne and the monarchy was abandoned, and that in 1969 the monarchy of King Idriss I of Libya was terminated by a military coup. But, in contrast, the monarchy of Morocco, which has some centuries of history behind it and is also related to the religious leadership of the country, alone survived in North Africa.

The educated people of the whole coast preach a radical and socialist doctrine which varies only in degree from person to person and place to place, and the uninstructed foreigner might justifiably consider them first-class fodder for communism. There are, in fact, few genuine communists to be found in North Africa. The radical or socialist content of Arab nationalism stems naturally from the great contrasts of wealth and poverty which exist everywhere in the region, and in the beginning it was not concerned with theoretical concepts of

socialism, but with the need to acquire the skills and techniques and education of the western world in order to create the wealth which would raise the standards of living of the masses. This was true of Egypt as recently as 1952, when the revolutionary government pledged its whole future on the High Dam at Aswan.

Russia's power in Egypt is not to be confused with communist influence, which has always been minimal. The Egyptian people as a whole dislike the commitment to Russia and would gladly get rid of it if they could secure economic aid on the scale required for the progress of the country and the arms necessary to resist Israel. Algeria, the other North African country once closely associated with Russia, is weakening the links largely because oil makes her economically less dependent, because she is not threatened by Israel, and can get her military hardware from France. It is need, not ideological commitment, that leads Arab peoples to Russia.

Yet there remains a great reservoir of poverty throughout the region. There are about 75 million inhabitants, of whom 40 million live in the Nile Valley in Egypt and the Sudan and about 27 million in Algeria and Morocco, and despite industrialization and oil production the majority of these people lives modestly on the proceeds of agriculture and, to a small extent, fishing. Even in Libya, which has a population of only 2 million and in eight years has become the third largest oil producer in the world, the benefits of oil wealth have not yet reached the mass of the people, of whom 30 percent are still nomadic and seminomadic. The most balanced economy is that of Algeria which exports crude oil, iron ore, phosphates, wine, citrus and soft fruits, but one-third of the total revenue still comes from agriculture. Egypt has industrialized extensively since the revolution of 1952, but it still depends mainly on cotton and the textile industry developed from it and has not been able to keep pace with the growth of population, which runs at the rate of about 750,000 a year, despite the Aswan High Dam. Industrial centers throughout the region are urban pockets in what is still a largely agricultural and nomadic world, and it will require vast amounts of capital and many decades of planning before life in North Africa is changed.

Until that time comes, the region will remain a strange world of contrasts despite the dynamics of radical Arab "socialism." The great cities like Cairo, Tripoli, Tunis, Rabat, and Casablanca are centers of sophistication, where the impact of western life has been strongest and the social tenets of Islam have been most weakened. Here the foreigner meets a way of life not vastly different from his own and among the languages spoken there is usually one that he can speak himself; but as he moves out from the centers of the cities he comes closer to the nature of older societies that predated the coming of the Europeans; there he finds customs, beliefs, and monuments of great antiquity which still color the lives of the people and are only slowly altered by the passage of time.

9 SOUTH AFRIC.

WHERE WHITE IS MIGHT

the white-dominated Republic of South Africa (471,445 square miles) is the most powerful and advanced country in Africa. But it consolidates its strength—and incidentally outrages most of the rest of the world—by openly and unashamedly operating under a policy of *apartheid,* a repressive denial of the civil and human rights of all people under its jurisdiction who are not accepted as white.

Politically, *apartheid*—backed by the power of a modern army and air force and paramilitary police—helps the government to perpetuate control over a large trust territory and to cement its alliance with racist Rhodesia. *Apartheid* also fuels the hatred of Africa's black states.

Economically it means fabulous profit from the sweat of underpaid, indentured black labor.

Socially it means a dual pattern of white and black life, implemented by an almost paranoid system of complex legal sanctions.

Technically, *apartheid* means no more than "separateness"; in practice it is the severe and absolute racial segregation of blacks and coloreds from whites, which is officially rationalized as an opportunity for self-determination. "*Apartheid,*" Balthazar Johannes Vorster, South Africa's Prime Minister, has said, "provides for the separate political development of the various distinctive peoples who go to make up our multinational population."

Vorster's is the bland and righteous voice of the men in power, the proponent of a creed explicable only in terms of a perverted evolution of the Calvinist attitudes brought to South Africa by Dutch pioneers in 1652, and symbolized today by the stern, gray-brown Voortrekker Monument near Pretoria. The sides of the monument, which is a national shrine, sweep up from a huge square base to a narrowing, slit-windowed top. It commemorates the epic trek of 1835, when the Boer (farmer) Afrikaners—descendants of the early Dutch, German, and French Huguenot settlers whose heirs now constitute 60 percent of the nation's white population—quit the British-ruled Cape Colony in covered oxwagons to resettle on virgin lands in the north. Sculptures around the monument portray aspects of Afrikaner history. The stone figures of men are hard-eyed, leathery, and bushy-bearded. Thin, bonneted women and their children are shown as prisoners in British concentration camps during the Boer War (Afrikaners call it "the English War"). The voortrekker wagons are encircled by hordes of yelling black savages. The friezes speak of struggle and determination, of privation and steely rigidity, of reliance on both Bible and *sjambok* (rhino-hide whip).

These rigorous memories are deeply lodged in the Afrikaner psyche. This is a white who considers himself an African as much as any black man, and who holds that the land settled by his forebears—although they were aliens and *uitlanders*—is legitimately and unquestionably his. He has never doubted his right to own, control, and

220

rule the country. He has always insisted that he understands its needs and interests better than outsiders, among whom he includes his South African neighbors, the British. Their wavering policy of well-intentioned idealism and self-serving voracity, formulated half a world away in London, was no match for Afrikaner single-mindedness, and eventually the Afrikaner wrested away British power and destroyed British influence. Now he is free to wage his "holy war" of survival against the overwhelming mass of black men. He claims to administer *apartheid* by divine right and points to the Old Testament to prove that blacks are destined to remain hewers of wood and drawers of water.

One travels about the sunny Republic of South Africa trying to fathom the deep roots of its dilemma: a land rich in precious gems and vital metals, yet impoverished in spirit. One realizes that the rarest commodities in South Africa are humanity and a sense of reality.

The first thing that impresses about South African cities is their size and western air. The highways are filled with late-model American, British, and continental cars. The buildings rise ever higher—factories, generating plants, skyscraper blocks—and everywhere there are monstrous yellow construction cranes.

But then the visitor senses a sulphurous tension. The atmosphere, as one touring American editor described it, is "filled with the corruption of fear." For all his material wealth, the grim-faced South African white man does not look happy. His home is heavily burglar-barred, and one of the fortunes to be made in South Africa is in household alarm-bell equipment.

One of the few whites in South Africa who is outspokenly opposed to *apartheid* is Dr. Bruckner de Villiers, a remarkable and courageous man with a shock of silver-black hair and an impeccable family pedigree. If anyone qualifies as South African on the basis of background, Dr. de Villiers does. But he is a renegade. "Whites and non-whites must live and rule together," he has said, and for such heretical thoughts he is an outcast from the clergy of the all-powerful Dutch Reformed Church, which unites religious authority and political power to a degree unknown in most other countries of the world. He is now a leader of an insurgent group, the Christian Institute, which has no church affiliation, but serves as a rallying point for people who share Dr. de Villiers' convictions.

"My fellow Afrikaner is a man in revolt against himself," Dr. de Villiers has said. "He is being tugged both ways, torn apart. On the one hand, he's got these chauvinist instincts, his nationalist instincts. This is a very strong instinct, not only with the Afrikaner, but with any people.

"On the other hand, he has got his Christian concepts which tell him that the way his national instinct is driving him is not the way Christ would have commanded.

"The Afrikaner is a con-

221

Handclaps signal beginning of dance of males of Bushman clan. Hunters (below) are armed with primitive bows, shoot poison-tipped arrows. Environment is rigorous, but Bushman life is not arduous. Bottom: Contemporary picture recalls 1835 Boer trek across South African veld.

fused man. He can make decisions which to the outside world, I suppose, would appear completely illogical. The Afrikaner fears. He fears division in his own ranks. He fears the English, the English usurper, the English intruder. . . . He fears the black man. He fears himself. He fears his own conscience."

Dr. de Villiers' fellow Afrikaners, as self-styled defenders of Christian civilization, rank among the world's most devout churchgoers. The Dutch Reformed Church, however, not only condones *apartheid*, but endorses it with the full vigor of its tremendous influence and practices it with separate white, African, and Colored branches. The latter are termed "daughter" churches and they teach small, nonwhite parishioners to call the saints "Baas Peter" and "Baas Paul."

But men like de Villiers represent the best in the Afrikaner character. There is independence there, the kind of brave independence that took the Afrikaners across a thousand miles of wilderness on the Great Trek. There is doggedness there, the kind that enabled the Boers to wage war against the mighty British empire, to outfight the enemy with cunning and fortitude until overcome by the weight of superior numbers and superior arms. And there is some conscience there. Dr. de Villiers and a few others testify to it.

The support of the many average white men for government policy is well expressed by a stocky Afrikaner rancher outside Aliwal North, on the northern border of Cape Province. His name is Stephanus Bekker. He has served in Parliament. His natural language is Afrikaans, the bastardized Dutch which is South Africa's official language. He believes with peasant fervor in his inflexible Calvinist God, and he has no doubts that God believes in him.

Bekker stood on a narrow shelf of rock that had pin-style Bushmen paintings at least a thousand years old on the walls below the overhang. He called attention to the paintings with some pride—even though his father had hunted Bushmen like rabbits because they could not distinguish between game animals and the Bekkers' cattle.

"There were lions and elephant and eland here before we came," said Bekker. "We cleared the land. We made it yield through good years and bad. If you don't understand us, let us alone. Let us alone for a hundred years and every man in South Africa, black and white, will be happy."

He waved his arm over the veld. "This is my land. It belonged to my father and to my grandfather. It will belong to my sons and to my grandsons. My grandfather came here in 1826. We have been here a long time, and we are going to be here a long time."

In this kind of persistence there is little consideration of, and little room for, blacks. And although there are some 14 to 16 million of them, as opposed to 4 million whites of Boer or British stock, they are kept segregated.

Any sensible man realizes that talk of permanently separating the races reflects a distorted dream of unscrambling the omelette. So the extreme measures of the government to keep the races separate border on mania. For instance, the beautiful beaches of South Africa—with the Atlantic on the west coast and the Indian Ocean on the east—are divided into sections extending far out into the water for each of the four racial groups: the whites, Cape Coloreds, Asians, and Africans. Japanese visitors, because of the business wealth they generally represent, are classed as "honorary whites" and given all the attendant privileges. South Africa's eight thousand resident Chinese, however, are obliged to remain in the shadow of the *apartheid* wall, although South Africa has considerable covert trade with Peking (which, in turn, arms and trains bands of anti-South African black guerrillas in neighboring countries).

In the crowded black townships outside the white urban centers, population and crime increase sharply. The government talks about "influx control," and year by year lengthens the list of its oppressive laws.

The big township of Soweto, on the outskirts of Johannesburg, is typical of the way black workers are concentrated in contemporary South Africa. About 800,000 African men, women, and children are packed into it, a third of them probably illegal lodgers toward whom the hard-pressed authorities simply turn a blind eye. Soweto is the scene of a thousand murders a year, mostly by "tsotsis," ruthless black gangsters who prey on their own people.

Ironically, the people of Soweto live better, in material terms, than most blacks outside South Africa. Government officials are fond of telling the visitor "their" Africans own more cars than the Russians. They do. And the medical and educational facilities available to some of them are on a par with those offered the communist masses. (Information on the high rate of infant malnutrition in rural areas is not so readily volunteered.)

Like Russia, the Republic of South Africa has made a tall, barbed-wire fence of its legal system. One example: no African may remain in an urban area for more than seventy-two hours without permission, unless he was born there and has lived there continuously thereafter; or has worked for one employer for a period of ten years, and remained there continuously thereafter; or has been there continuously for fifteen years working for no more than one employer, and has continued to live there thereafter. A wife, or an unmarried daughter or son under the age of eighteen, may get permission to live in an urban area with an African who is a husband or father if they can prove that they ordinarily reside with him and that they entered the area lawfully.

All black workers are tagged merely as "temporary sojourners" in South Africa's urban areas, and an Afrikaner administrator

Underside of South Africa: Zulu rickshaw man is descendent of warriors who fought British and Boers. N'debele mother and son. Bottom: In and outside of Xhosa huts in Transkei enclave, where blacks are supposed to prove a capacity for self-development. Opposite: A Pretoria street boy.

of the Orange Free State refers to black wives and children in South Africa's towns as "superfluous." Families are broken up by rubber stamps.

The Africans must carry brown pass books, with head-and-shoulders photographs, at all times or they are liable to arrest. The book details where the holder can live, where he or she works (with the employer's signature as confirmation), or where the holder can look for employment. If the book is not properly signed or stamped, the holder is in danger of being behind bars within an hour of being picked up. Pass raids by baton-brandishing police squads on townships and overcrowded native buses and trains in the Johannesburg area alone net 700,000 victims a year.

Black and liberal opposition to the South African regime has been stamped out with torture, life-long prison terms and elaborate trials for treason in the courts. But the opening of a recent major trial in Pretoria High Court under the Terrorism Act—which created new offenses and made them retroactive to 1962—was marked by a display of clenched fists, the defiant symbol of American black militants, from defendants in the dock. The incidents suggested that the country may one day experience the biggest Black Power problem ever seen. Some political detainees have been beaten to death (there were at least seven deaths of persons in custody during 1969), others forced to "confess" through severe electric shocks applied to the genitals and other parts of the body by police.

Under South African law, any person can be held indefinitely without charges or trial for questioning regarding widely-defined "terrorism" and other general matters connected with the security of the state. Under this Kafkaesque procedure, which frequently includes solitary confinement, a man might die in his cell without knowing exactly why he was there in the first place.

It is a criminal offense for more than twelve blacks to meet and talk together without official permission.

A person "named" under the Suppression of Communism—meaning, in essence, liberalism—Act cannot be quoted in a newspaper or through any other public media. He or she becomes a political zombie, one of the living dead.

At any one time, one in about forty South Africans—and most of them black —is in jail. According to official figures, half a million people were sentenced to imprisonment there in the year 1968-1969. More than 475,000 of these were blacks, many of whom had been arrested for technical offenses under the pass laws. In the same period, 25,933 "strokes of corporal punishment"—whip lashes—were administered throughout the land. South Africa's crime, auto accident, suicide, divorce, drunkenness, and execution rates (sixty-four persons —all Africans, Asians, and Coloreds—went to the scaffold in 1969) are among the highest in the world.

The right of blacks to own property is severely restricted. The average annual

228

income is $210, as opposed to $3,200 per capita for whites. They do not have the franchise; in spring, 1970, when a general election called by Premier Vorster was held, they stood by, silently and despondently, as whites went to the polls. Under such bondage, the blacks turn increasingly to the brotherly comfort of tribalism and turn away—defiantly whispering Black Power slogans—from the tepid warmth of the Christian churches. And the noted South African author, Alan Paton, asked whether his was a Nazi country, replied, "No, but it's a very good imitation of one."

Yet the booming economy of South Africa also mocks the creed of *apartheid*. The mining of diamonds ($150 million per year) and gold (72 percent of the western world's yearly supply) could not be carried on without black workers. The big cities would be paralyzed without them. South Africa's gross national product has doubled in a decade. More and more blacks are needed to maintain the pace of prosperity under a political system which tries to shut them out. Nearly 90,000 new industrial jobs open up each year and, even with encouragement of large-scale white immigration, there are not nearly enough whites to fill them. Under the work laws skilled and semiskilled posts are reserved for whites, but evasions are winked at everywhere.

The Vorster government's insistence on imposing strict *apartheid* on the country's labor-hungry industry has brought it into open conflict with Harry Oppenheimer, one of the ten richest men in the world, who is a leading opponent among South Africa's businessmen of racial separation. His companies, including the giant Anglo-American Corporation, dig the gold and diamonds and minerals out of the South African earth and were inherited from his father who helped to build Johannesburg, the "City of Gold."

Oppenheimer, whom Afrikaner cartoonists depict as a tubby, bejewelled "Hoggenheimer," says: "While politicians have been preaching *apartheid*, the businessmen have been busy with a massive economic development which has been based on ever-increasing integration of the races. . . . Far too many people in southern Africa think that civilized means the same thing as white. Well, it doesn't. Quite clearly we've got to get away in this matter from racial discrimination. One's got to find some better criterion to decide what makes a man civilized." He adds gravely: "I realize I am living in a country which is politically a failure."

Nonetheless, Vorster has declared that, despite enforced easing of job discrimination, the rigors of social *apartheid* will continue to be applied. He predicts total residential segregation by 1977. "No pressure from whatever source," he said after a recent election returned his National Party to power, "will force the government to abandon the *apartheid* policy." In Vorster's view the five main tasks facing the nation are:

1) To stabilize race relations on the basis of separate racial development.

2) To build the infrastructure for further rapid economic and other development of the country.

3) To strengthen South Africa's ties with friendly overseas countries "on the understanding they must accept us as we are."

4) To keep the country militarily prepared and economically strong.

5) For South Africans to steel themselves to withstand "moral degeneration" throughout the world.

Under Point 1, the blacks of South Africa—the whites call them Bantus, which is actually a linguistic designation—are supposed to develop independently under a delusory Bantustan system, which is a relentless social and political program, and the proclaimed future of *apartheid.*

"A Bantustan or, as we prefer to call it, a Bantu homeland, is really a potential independent black state in South Africa and South-West Africa which will eventually become independent," the government has said in a typical statement. "The intention is to have eight or so of these Bantu homelands. Thirteen percent of the republic will be set aside for the main tribes to live in and rule fundamentally. We are busy with a program of industrialization of the homelands and the areas bordering them. We have during the last few years invested—through private initiative, through private industry, and through the Industrial Development Corporation, which is a semigovernment or-

ganization—over $10 million in developing the fringes of these Bantustans."

Along those border areas, according to theory, white-owned factories can be set up, and new industries for the profit of the white man can grow.

The stony, dusty, and undeveloped Transkei, 16,000 square miles in the east of South Africa, is the first of these Bantustans. With its patchworks of agricultural smallholdings and clusters of beehive-style huts, it has been the designated homeland of 3.5 million Xhosa tribespeople since December, 1963. Others, for big tribes such as the Zulus and the Tswana, are still only in the formative stages, or on theoreticians' drawing boards. The basically powerless Transkei is an expensive piece of fiction presented as black independence. The reality is that the Bantustan is merely a well-fenced combination of a reservoir of fresh African labor and a dumping ground from the urban areas of the old and unwanted of a particular tribe.

No white South African leader will give the Xhosas or any other tribe a taste of true democracy. It would be dangerous if they should learn to like it. Asked what would happen if the Transkei went communist, a government spokesman contemplated the fantastic suggestion and then retorted: "Our armored cars would soon deal with the situation."

Meanwhile, the ranks of the 4 million blacks who work in urban areas are

Pure molten gold pouring into ingots (far left) marks end and purpose of black miners' effort in their underworld labyrinths. Mine dumps, residue of years of operation, rise ever higher on Johannesburg outskirts. Above ground, all-white members play lawn bowls at Wanderers' Club.

being swollen regularly by the arrival of new crowds of so-called migrant labor.

About 614,000 Asians and some 2 million Cape Coloreds (half-castes) also suffer grievously under *apartheid*. Although there are distinctions among the disadvantaged which place them on different levels of the social and economic scales, many of their leaders have in the past found common cause with the blacks against tyranny. For there are few rights denied to Africans which are given to the Asians and Cape Coloreds. The latter groups have comparatively better access to higher education (where the fees can be met), but in sum is still inadequate. Although a greater number of these nonwhites are able to afford more stylish, less stereotyped homes than blacks, they too are unable to share the white man's cabs, his hospitals, his churches, his buses and trains, his telephone boxes, and his cafes (although, like Africans, the Asians and Coloreds can be served food to take away at sidewalk hatches). All are barred, too, from sexual intercourse with a white person, which is proscribed by the Immorality Act and punished by heavy prison sentences to both parties. Couples who married across the color line before 1949, when it still was legal to do so, have been forced apart or made "untouchables" by the current Prohibition of Mixed Marriages Act.

The Asians, principally Indians, first came to South Africa in 1860 as indentured laborers on the Natal sugar plantations under an arrangement sponsored by the British colonial government. Their numbers were later supplemented

Black Johannesburg wears a less cheerful aspect than white. Coal deliverers (opposite) are in ranks of menial labor. Mine recruits (below) await train transport to company compounds where they will live for duration of work contract. City bargain stores attract both blacks and whites.

by others who came from India on their own account as traders, craftsmen, and merchants. Asians, who now include doctors, architects, and lawyers, and are to be found in the Transvaal and the Cape as well as Natal, are subject to commercial and residential segregation. The Coloreds—"God's stepchildren"—who are the descendants of unions between the indigenous Hottentot tribespeople of the Cape and the white pioneers, are also trapped by the Afrikaner mentality in a designated district of the gracious city of Capetown. For many years the English dominated the Cape Province, and Capetown's lovely white, yellow, and brown buildings and wide boulevards lined with flowering trees suggest a more expansive spirit than that which pervades the rest of the country. The mother city of South Africa is also known as "the tavern of the seas," and the doomed "Flying Dutchman" is reputed to sail endlessly off its rocky shores.

South African government officials protest that anybody with even a little Negro blood in his veins remains a Negro in America, while in their country "if a man appears to be white and lives in accordance with white standards we ac-

cept him as white, and no more questions are asked."

The important word in that statement is "appears" because appearance is written into the law. And it is remarkable how white a child can appear when his parents are important. A number of South African politicians are obviously of mixed blood; hence the gruesome mockery of their bitter fight to preserve the "white race." There are "pass-for-white" children at almost any Boer fete throughout South Africa and no one objects to them. Quite a few "white" South Africans could walk through Harlem as if they belonged.

But recently—as has happened in hundreds of other such tragic cases—the daughter of an Afrikaner farmer was told she had been classified as "Colored." This fateful decision was based on the arbitrary verdict of a white civil servant. (Sometimes a pencil is run through a person's hair to see if he or she has any of the tight, crinkly curls of the Bantu.) Consequently the girl could not live in her father's house as his daughter—only, the law decrees, as a servant.

Geneticists say that any white South African who can trace his origins in that country back more than two hundred years is almost certain to have mixed blood; and these are members of the country's aristocracy.

Pigmentation apart, under British rule most Afrikaners were poor whites engaged in a fierce struggle for existence. By now they have won control of a very important piece of the world's real estate, and they are not about to let go.

Today South Africa even has other countries serving her as economic serfs— the black countries of Botswana, Lesotho, and Swaziland. Until 1966 these were the three British High Commission territories in southern Africa. They had come into being because native leaders in Queen Victoria's time sought the protection of the crown (they called it "the Queen's blanket") against warring neighbors and rapacious whites arriving from the old Cape Colony. The original intention of the British was to incorporate the High Commission territories into South Africa. But when the National Party defeated General Jan Christian Smuts' United Party and took power after World War II, the *apartheid* structure was established and all notions of incorporating black regions and populations in South Africa died.

Botswana, larger than Texas, is encircled by South Africa, South-West Africa, Portugal's Angola, and Rhodesia. Near the magnificent Victoria Falls in the north a fingertip of Botswana touches the independent black state of Zambia, (formerly Northern Rhodesia), which is a top producer of copper.

Landlocked Botswana (225,000 square miles) has a scrawny cattle-and-dairy economy, dry-mouthed from lack of water. In this arid region more than half a million Africans, including the "Stone Age" little Bushmen of the Kalahari Desert, and four thousand whites (most of them

South Africans) work out a way of living together. Despite independence, those whites still guide Botswana economically, with the obligatory co-operation of the black leaders. Sir Seretse Khama, a descendant of warrior kings, who became the country's first president at independence, openly rejects the *apartheid* policies of South Africa, but is geographically forced to trade the bulk of Botswana's cattle and hides with her. Botswana, with newly discovered copper, diamond, and nickel deposits, maintains active relations with Zambia and regards herself as something of a bridge, however narrow, between the white-governed countries of the south and the northern black states.

Rugged Lesotho (11,716 square miles) is a tiny island in the vast "white sea" of the Republic of South Africa. There are roughly a million Bantu in Lesotho, which has been described as "the beleaguered last outpost of black Africa," and about two thousand whites—again chiefly South Africans. About half of Lesotho's adult male population spends years working in the mines and factories of South Africa. The men return to their homeland with natty new suits, leather briefcases, sunglasses, and gleaming, tinny wristwatches after their lonely spell of duty is over. Without this migrant labor system, Lesotho would be in dire trouble. But the South African labor market can have frightening and depressing effects on the families of the men of Lesotho (and Botswana and Swaziland). The absence of menfolk prevents the country from developing the agri-cultural economy on which it must grow. More importantly, it means women without husbands, children without fathers, and parents without support—fractured family units everywhere.

Africa is a wild combination of natural richness and natural poverty. In Lesotho the poverty coexists with an abundant natural resource—water. The broad Orange river, vital to South Africa, originates among Lesotho's snowcapped mountains where pagoda-hatted tribesmen riding wiry ponies may stumble upon large diamonds. Here was an obvious place to develop hydroelectric power which could be used throughout Lesotho and South Africa, particularly the southern Transvaal industrial complex, and this has now been done through a $60 million project financed by South Africa.

Lush little Swaziland (6,705 square miles), an independent tribal monarchy since September, 1968, is richer and more sparsely populated than Lesotho. The lovely miniature kingdom of misty peaks, pineapple plantations, trout streams, and clusters of black-clay African huts dotting the green lowlands is one of the more peaceful countries in all Africa. The vain and handsome Swazi warriors, who dye their mop-like hair brown with iron-ore solutions from ancient mines, invariably carry shaving mirrors into which they peer at frequent intervals. Living among, and in effect controlling, nearly half a million Swazis are ten thousand whites (about three-quarters of them hardy citizens of the South African republic) who are administra-

tive officers, teachers, farmers, missionaries, and merchants. Most black families live off a marginal agrarian economy. The climate and soil of Swaziland are good, the water plentiful, and the mineral resources impressive. It exports iron ore, sugar, wood pulp, and fruit. In 1970, President Nixon offered assistance to Swaziland to underscore his disapproval of *apartheid*.

South-West Africa is the oldest *apartheid* appendage of South Africa. Known as Namibia at the UN, it is more than half the size of the Republic itself. In the First World War, South African troops defeated the German forces in South-West Africa, which was then one of the Kaiser's colonies. The League of Nations in 1919 granted the territory to South Africa as a mandate, and the League's statesmen spoke piously of the deal as "a sacred trust of civilization." South African politicians, however, simply regarded the land as war booty, and in the same year they took it over in that light. Draconian laws were passed later to preserve the white South African grip on land and mineral rights. More recently, the United Nations, with a growing membership of non-white states, has tried to call South Africa to account. South Africa insists that the United Nations is not the legal successor to the defunct League of Nations and has no authority over the South-West mandate. Until force of arms alters the situation, the 318,261 square miles that make up South-West Africa and the three-quarters of a million people (only sixty thousand of them white) who live there will be subject to the will of Pretoria.

What South Africa rules is a barren coastal zone that rises to several plateaus, equally barren. Why should anyone want South-West? Well, diamonds in plenty were discovered on its "Skeleton Coast" in 1908. There are also some important mineral deposits, and a good international market for the skins of the large karakul-sheep flocks.

South-West Africa, with its strong Boer and ex-German population, echoes the race policies of South Africa. The administrator of South-West Africa is an Afrikaner who tells the visitor what he will hear all over South Africa itself. "All the different racial groups have money in their pockets and hope in their hearts," he says with poker-faced piety. But then he tells grimly of the raids on his territory by armed bands of black freedom fighters —"terrorists and saboteurs," he calls them—from the springboards of Zambia and northern Botswana. These guerrilla incursions have been going on for years, in increasing intensity, as part of the overall struggle for the liberation of southern Africa.

South-West Africa is a long-established situation *vis-à-vis* South Africa, but in the Republic of Rhodesia (150,820 square miles), where a quarter of a million whites hold sway over 5 million Africans, the Afrikaner state has a new junior partner and an enthusiastic spiritual ally.

The white men of South Africa and Rhodesia have always seen majority rule as a disaster, as leading to the destruction of western civilization in the two countries. Cecil John Rhodes, the adventurous nineteenth-century British founder of what became Southern and Northern Rhodesia, was less hypocritical. True, he claimed that the colonization of southern Africa in the last century was a white philanthropic effort, but he quickly added that "philanthropy plus five percent" was much better than philanthropy alone.

As Zambia and small, poor Nyasaland (now Malawi) approached independence in 1964, after years as uneasy partners with Southern Rhodesia in the Central African Federation, the attitude of white Southern Rhodesians hardened over the issue of controlling their own racial policies. African and world political pressure compelled Britain to refuse Southern Rhodesia's demands for full independence (which were not coupled with any undertaking that the country's black majority—albeit politically inexperienced and tribally divided—would ever be permitted to take eventual control). "The whites have racial partnership on their lips," an African leader in Salisbury said at the time, "and *apartheid* in their hearts."

In November, 1965, the Rhodesian Prime Minister, Ian Smith, issued a unilateral declaration of independence (U.D.I.). He had the wholehearted support of the brawny whites, and socialist Great Britain refused to challenge the declaration militarily. Instead, economic sanctions were invoked which were largely ineffectual.

Tobacco (Rhodesia's main cash crop), asbestos, chrome, coal, and copper remained primary productions as South Africa and international corporations aided and abetted the rebels in their evasion of subsequent UN embargoes. Tobacco farmers who sent their bales to secret auctions in Salisbury received guaranteed prices per pound from the Smith government.

The true white Rhodesian's attitudes are expressed by Smith, who gave his U.D.I. over the radio with a tasteless parody of the American Declaration of Independence.

Early in 1970, as African freedom forces continued to infiltrate Rhodesia from across the Zambezi in dugout canoes, Smith severed his last, frayed ties with Britain and her queen by naming Rhodesia a republic. In March of the same year he held an election on the *apartheid* ticket, and won all fifty, white-elected seats in Parliament.

Its system was never robustly democratic, but Rhodesia—before Smith and U.D.I. brought an end to her thirty-two years as a self-governing colony of Britain—had at one time planted a few seeds of racial concord with limited political and social overlapping. The seeds have now withered in the imported soil of *apartheid*. Rhodesia's Land Tenure Act and other measures enforce "chessboard" segregation, with the whites owning the richest farmlands and occupying exclusively the best business and residential areas in the cities and towns. The republican constitution inaugurated by Smith bars Rhodesia's blacks (with all their political principals held under restriction for years without trial) from ever attaining majority rule.

White Rhodesia, fronting a noisily hostile African north, draws comfort from the strong and ever-ready military forces of her political and economic suzerain, South Africa. Although no blood brothers of Ian Smith and his fellow "Engelsmen," South Africa's Afrikaners would not turn their backs if Rhodesia were attacked by black armies. Vorster's well-armed security forces, using armored cars and helicopters, have long been aiding the Rhodesian army in beating back guerrilla forays. Thus, Rhodesia has had to come quickly into line with unadulterated *apartheid* and to swallow hard her dependency status as regards both tanks and trade.

There is an old Ghanaian proverb which warns, "If you are in hiding, don't light a fire." White-ruled southern Africa, which consists of the republics of Vorster and Smith, South-West Africa, and the Portuguese "provinces" of Angola and Mozambique, is a society trying to hide amid numerous fires.

The whites are incredibly sensitive to the judgments the *uitlanders* make about them. But the vast majority is unwilling to respond to those judgments with any tangible change. Concerning the question of minority rule and suppression of the blacks, the whites argue wide cultural differences, population imbalance, the virtues of separate development, and the "cruelty" of forcing the black man to compete openly with his pale-skinned counterpart. Various ethnic, theological, historical, and sociological arguments are put forward to bolster the case. Yet what it really amounts to is that the white man down in this part of Africa has a very good life at the expense of the blacks. And he is determined to retain his power and profit as long as he can.

In consequence of hostile world opinion, these white-run states of southern Africa regard themselves as besieged countries—besieged from without and within—which cannot afford such luxuries of democracy as free expression. Like tycoons making handsome profits who boast of their "service" to a community, the whites of the south claim they have brought progress and civilization to the black multitudes. International big business turns a blind eye to the cynical charade.

The average black in southern Africa who is kept at a subsistence level of life in his own land and denied any effective political rights remains unimpressed by this boast. He says he would sooner starve in freedom than eat in chains and points scornfully to a white civilization which has produced two disastrous world wars within his memory.

On the other hand, the free millions of black Africa will not be content until their brothers acquire freedom in the southern part of the continent. And they will not fully trust any Western nation until it gets actively behind their efforts to force the "white man boss" off their soil at the tip of Africa.

PICTURE CREDITS

INDEX

Picture references in italics